AIRFIX

magazine guide 25

Modelling World War 2 Fighters

Bryan Philpott

Patrick Stephens Ltd
in association with Airfix Products Ltd

First published — 1977

ISBN 0 85059 262 3

Cover design by Tim McPhee

Text set in 8 on 9 pt Univers Medium
by Stevenage Printing Limited,
Stevenage.
Printed in Great Britain on Fineblade
cartridge 90 gsm and bound by the
Garden City Press, Letchworth,
Herts.
Published by Patrick Stephens
Limited, Bar Hill, Cambridge, CB3 8EL,
in association with Airfix Products
Limited, London SW18.

Don't forget these other Airfix Magazine Guides!

No 1 *Plastic Modelling*
No 2 *Aircraft Modelling*
No 3 *Military Modelling*
No 4 *Napoleonic Wargaming*
No 5 *Tank & AFV Modelling*
No 6 *RAF Fighters of World War 2*
No 7 *Warship Modelling*
No 8 *German Tanks of World War 2*
No 9 *Ancient Wargaming*
No 10 *Luftwaffe Camouflage
of World War 2*
No 11 *RAF Camouflage
of World War 2*
No 12 *Afrika Korps*
No 13 *The French Foreign Legion*
No 14 *American Fighters
of World War 2*
No 15 *World War 2 Wargaming*
No 16 *Modelling Jet Fighters*
No 17 *British Tanks of World War 2*
No 18 *USAAF Camouflage
of World War 2*
No 19 *Model Soldiers*
No 20 *8th Army in the Desert*
No 21 *Modelling Armoured Cars*
No 22 *Russian Tanks of World War 2*
No 23 *German Fighters
of World War 2*
No 24 *American Civil War Wargaming*
No 26 *American Tanks of World War 2*

Contents

Acknowledgements

I should like to acknowledge the help given by many modellers, societies, museums and aircraft manufacturers especially, John Carter, John Whalley, Mike Silk, Dave Howely, Tony Woollet, members of the Berkshire, Essex and Sheffield branches of the IPMS, the RAF Museum, the Imperial War Museum, the Royal Air Force, the United States Air Force, British Aircraft Corporation, the Fleet Air Arm Museum, Hawker Siddeley Aviation Ltd, and the editor of *Airfix Magazine;* Martin Holbrook, who once again turned his talents to the production of the drawings, his father, Lieutenant Commander D.A.E. Holbrook RN (Retd) who was particularly helpful with information about the Seafire, and last but by no means least, John Beaman.

Dedicated to Simon and Mark

Editor's introduction

Amongst plastic construction kit subjects, fighter aircraft of World War 2 are unquestionably still the most popular. More modellers probably begin their hobby by making a Spitfire than any other kit, and this aircraft's popularity is duly reflected in the large number of variants available from practically every manufacturer under the sun. However, kits vary in quality, not least of all through their age, and the modeller who intends taking his hobby seriously will soon discover shortcomings in even the most up to date kits. Most of these can be rectified using the methods outlined in this book and the same author's previous *Airfix Magazine Guide* on basic aircraft modelling, number 2 in the series. Similarly, older kits which the serious modeller may tend to neglect as unworthy of his attention can be improved and brought up to modern standards by careful work and detailing.

The aim of this book is to show, through practical examples, some of the potential for improving and detailing Airfix fighter kits both old and new, and how alternative variants can be added to a collection through cross-kitting and converting.

The subjects covered include Seafires, night-fighting Corsairs, a Japanese Zero on floats and many other models which can be converted with a little thought and patience. The kits on which these conversions are based range from the Airfix Zero, which is one of the oldest offerings in their range, to the Messerschmitt Me 163, one of the very latest. However, there is not one which cannot be improved by the serious modeller, and even if none of the subjects covered are your own 'thing', the techniques and modifications described will prove invaluable in planning and executing your own models.

Cockpit detail is one particular area where attention is usually greatly rewarded, and in addition to showing how simple modifications can be made to improve this, Bryan Philpott has also included a useful guide to cockpit interior colours, a subject which baffles many modellers and spoils otherwise excellent models. Reshaping components, removing over-heavy surface detail, detailing and improving the shapes of items such as airscrews, spinners, exhausts, guns, canopies and undercarriage parts are all covered, providing an invaluable object lesson in what can be achieved with a little patience. But modelling is meant to be fun, and none of the work described is beyond the capabilities of the average modeller with a few kits beneath his belt — it is not for experts only. So get cracking!

BRUCE QUARRIE

one

Guidelines

Although sweeping generalisations can be dangerous, it is fairly safe to say that models of fighter aeroplanes are the most popular subjects among both serious and casual followers of the hobby of constructing plastic kits. This argument is supported and proved by even the most casual analysis of catalogues produced by the major manufacturers of plastic kits, a good example being that of the latest Airfix catalogue — the 13th at the time of writing — in which over 70 of the 200-odd 1:72 scale kits listed are of aircraft that can readily be identified in this category. Depending on the parameters of the definition used by the individual, this number could be increased by the inclusion of aircraft that were not primarily designed as fighters, but were at some time in their service careers pushed into action in this role.

Careful market research leads to the production of kits which will enjoy good sales, so it is clear that this must indicate a 'magic' surrounding fighter aircraft, which will ensure the high capital investment in tooling and design will be recovered and rewarded by good sales figures. There are perhaps hundreds of reasons why this type of aeroplane is attractive to modellers; these range from the important aspect of storage and display of the completed models, which are usually fairly small, to the glamour that surrounds the aircraft concerned, the exploits in which it has been involved, and the 'Walter Mitty' world to which most aviation enthusiasts occasionally retire, wherein their own skills as a fighter pilot

will match Ball, von Richtofen, Johnson, Galland, and the latter day jet-jockeys of Korea and Vietnam.

Whatever the reason, fighters are good modelling subjects and will continue to be so. It is not surprising, therefore, that those who endeavour to make a collection which tells a story often base this on fighter aircraft of a particular period, a campaign such as the Battle of Britain, or the development of one particular type. A simple theme based on the progression from biplane to supersonic jet would not be difficult, while similarly a collection showing the aircraft used by a particular squadron would also be effective and require comparatively little space for display. But as the horizons widen, any modeller who attempts this type of collection must first ask himself some searching questions.

One of the most important of these will be the availability of suitable reference material, which will be closely followed by an appraisal of the number of models commercially available, and how many of these can be converted to other marks or even completely different subjects. An important factor to take into consideration is the one of boredom. With the number of kits of the ubiquitous Spitfire now available, it would be possible to produce every mark of this famous fighter as well as many sub-types and experimental versions; a quick census of types and available kits indicates that over 60 types of Spitfire and Seafire could be produced without duplication! However much one loves the Spitfire, this would be a mammoth task and at times frustration and boredom would almost certainly either bring an end to the project or a decline in standards.

Aircraft of World Wars 1 and 2 have been well documented so their exploits, design, and colour schemes can be readily obtained. In many respects World War 1 seems to be the poor relation as far as manufacturers are concerned, whereas World War 2 is well catered for in every aspect of modelling — especially as far as fighters are concerned.

The Airfix range is readily available

and offers a choice of models which, with care, and in some cases hard work, will enable even the most impecunious modeller to collect a good cross-section of fighter aircraft used by the combatants of World War 2. In many cases kits are now beginning to show their age both in quality of moulding and accuracy, but the fact that they still remain in the available list indicates the popularity of the subject. Other manufacturers offer more modern mouldings which can, of course, be used. But in modifying or correcting one of the older Airfix kits, there is not a great deal at stake financially, and the habit of working in plastic is cultivated; a habit that is essential if the hobby is to be followed seriously and in depth. In some cases it is not possible to correct all the errors which have crept in, and where this occurs I have been careful to point it out, but the final decision as to whether or not to compromise or go for another manufacturer's kit remains the prerogative of the reader.

The basic techniques in assembling any plastic model have already been dealt with in *Airfix Magazine Guides* 1 and 2, as well as *Making Model Aircraft* (PSL, 1976), so there is no point in going over these again in detail. But it is worth recapping the essentials, which are: careful use of polystyrene cement; checking the fit of parts before assembly; adding interior detail; attention to sanding join lines; filling gaps between components, and similarly filling any sink marks or moulding deficiences; a wash in warm water with a touch of detergent before painting; careful painting with good brushes and well-stirred paint; and meticulous care in application of decals/transfers.

A word or two on the final finish would not seem out of place as this is a subject which is often surrounded by controversy. Obviously the decision as to how any particular model is to look must remain with the individual modeller concerned. Some prefer a pristine factory finish, while at the other end of the scale there are those who want their models to look as though they have been in action or exposed to the elements. My own personal view is that a model looks more realistic if it is 'weathered' to an acceptable degree. Fighters were produced to fight; although they were not allowed to become too scruffy, they did have their paintwork patched or scratched, their camouflage became faded, and fuel or oil, often both, stained areas around the engine cowlings and fuel tanks. The art of achieving an acceptable degree of such wear must be cultivated, and a good watchword is underdone rather than overdone. Always try to keep in mind that the model you are making is to a very small scale, and blemishes added by you must be magnified many times to get them into perspective with the original. A scrape one inch long on the fuselage of a model Spitfire would be six feet on the real aircraft, and it is extremely doubtful if even the most hard-pressed ground crew would have allowed such a major blemish to appear on their aircraft. There is no substitute for study of photographs of an aircraft in the condition you are trying to simulate, followed by careful practice on scrap plastic or an old model.

Wear which occurs where paint is scraped from the aircraft, either by the crew entering it or service personnel removing panels, is best reproduced by applying silver paint or Rub 'n Buff in small areas before the final camouflage scheme is applied. Areas of the silver are then treated with a masking fluid which is removed when final painting is completed. This achieves a correct appearance of paint being rubbed off the original skin rather than the false impression which can be gained by dabbing areas of the finish with silver paint. Streaks from exhausts and around gun ports are best applied with a very thin wash of black paint or diluted Indian Ink, applied—if possible—with an airbrush. Such blemishes should be very delicate and not appear as areas of black paint as they so often do. This technique is one that does require a little practice and the temptation is always present to try just a little more.

Every modeller will eventually arrive at his own pet method of carrying out this type of work, so I will not try to lay down any hard and fast rules other than to recommend that a study is made of the methods already well documented; try them all and adjust them to suit your own needs.

Another age-old question that is almost certain to raise its ugly head is the one of camouflage patterns and colours. I am not for one moment suggesting that all that has been published should be totally ignored, but one must quickly learn to differentiate between what was officially specified and what was, in actual fact, carried out.

The governing authority of every air force did lay down strict procedures in relation to aircraft finishes. In many cases these were adhered to by the various manufacturers, but once the aircraft had been in service these rules were frequently ignored or adapted to meet local conditions. It is one thing for a chair-bound administrator to prepare a directive which states that a certain colour and type of paint will be used, and quite another when it comes to a harassed crew chief finding such paint on a forward airfield.

In many cases a compromise had to be reached and there is plenty of written and photographic evidence to prove that colours and schemes were often adapted to suit local conditions and available supplies.

Obviously it is necessary to take as much care as possible in authenticating a colour scheme, and I am not trying to suggest that any colour or idea that comes to mind can be applied to a model which is supposed to represent a service aircraft. But there is a certain amount of leeway and the modeller must learn not to become too sensitive if many of the 'by-the-book' experts criticise his efforts. Paints used during World War 2 tended to vary from manufacturer to manufacturer, and were subject to fading in certain climates. The serious follower of the hobby must research this subject thoroughly, and be prepared to form his own conclusions and stick to them through thick and thin. Two good examples of variations from what is

expected by those who stick rigidly to the book are worth quoting. One results from my own service in the Royal Air Force, during which I saw a Meteor NF 14 fitted with a starboard wing from another aircraft, the result being that the new wing had an entirely different camouflage pattern from the one it replaced, as well as having colours that were much darker than the rest of the airframe. This aircraft flew for many months in this state before it was re-sprayed, so during the time it operated with an 'odd' wing, it contravened all the text books! The second occurred during the research for this book when the pilot of the Seafire III conversion featured on pages 27-31 was discussing his particular aircraft with Martin Holbrook, who has provided all the illustrations. The pilot is, in fact, Martin's father and he has retained a very comprehensive collection of photographs and records of his service with the Fleet Air Arm. In trying to establish the correct colour scheme for the aircraft, the pilot was shown many colour chips and finally a model painted in the colours officially laid down. Every example brought a shake of the head. Eventually the model was repainted with the original colours considerably lightened on the top surfaces and darkened on the undersides, which brought an affirmative reply with the added comment that the particular Seafire concerned was so faded and weathered that the top surfaces really did appear as one colour. Even allowing for the passage of 30-odd years, one must accept that the pilot was right in his assessment, since the aircraft and period had left an indelible impression on his mind.

Examples such as this are always worth remembering if you are a modeller who wants to produce aircraft as they *were* rather than as they *should* have been. Both approaches are correct and the whole question finally boils down to one of personal preference. The main point remains that modelling should be a pleasurable hobby, and if you achieve this within the realms of reasonable authenticity, it has fulfilled its aim.

two

Gloster Gladiator

The Gloster Gladiator was the last of the biplane fighters to see service with Fighter Command, and although it reached the zenith of its career at the time of the Munich Crisis in 1938, some squadrons were still equipped with this agile aircraft at the outbreak of World War 2.

Outclassed by its opposition, the Gladiator was still able to give a good account of itself in combat and made more than its mark in the Norwegian, Western Desert and Malta campaigns. Because of its length of service the Gladiator enables the modeller to choose many colour schemes, ranging from the colourful pre-war markings to the more sombre schemes used during its active service.

One of the most famous actions involving the Gladiator was the defence of Malta, when three Sea Gladiators were pressed into service to defend the island. These three machines became known as 'Faith', 'Hope' and 'Charity', whether at the time of the campaign or

Completed model of Sea Gladiator N5519 as operated from Malta.

at a later date is still not clear and is, in any case, beyond the scope of this book. One of the aircraft involved in this action, 'R' N5519, can be made by following the conversion instructions and adding a dinghy pack with which it was for a while equipped, but alternatives in the more common RAF camouflage are basically identical and the modeller therefore has a wide choice when it comes to completing this ubiquitous aircraft.

The Airfix kit is one of the oldest in the range, and although more modern releases are available, turning the older kit into an acceptable model is a challenge which presents plenty of opportunities to try methods that will be useful in all types of conversions.

Before joining the fuselage halves together, remove the rudder and moulded pilot's head, at the same time opening the cockpit area to enable detailing to be carried out. Cut a new rudder from 30 thou plastic card and shape this to aerofoil section using the accompanying drawings. Rib detail must be added but this will be described later as it is also needed in other areas. A cockpit floor is made from plastic card and to the front of this is fitted a bulkhead which also serves as a locating point for the instrument panel. The latter is also made from plastic card and can be painted light grey with the instruments scribed in then picked out in silver and black paint. Alternatively, cut two panels from 10 thou plastic card, paint the rear one matt black, drill holes to represent instruments in the front one, then glue the two together. The instruments can then be scribed through the drilled holes and a drop of gloss varnish applied in the holes to represent glass. This is a very effective method of producing instrument panels and can, of course, be used on any type of model.

The seat is made from thin plastic card or writing paper and fitted with a safety harness made from strips of paper painted light brown with stitching and adjustment holes marked with a mapping pen. An alternative might be found in the spares box but this will invariably need the addition of plastic

Blenheim cowling

Gladiator L7616
94 Squadron RAF
Dark Earth and Dark Green with black
and Sky under surfaces (centre line division)

card sides to make it into a more authentic bucket seat of the type fitted to the Gladiator. The control column is the type with a circular grip at the top and is made from stretched sprue, the grip being fashioned around the pointed end of a cocktail stick whilst the sprue is still warm. At this stage it is a good idea to add internal structure to the cockpit with strips of thinly stretched sprue, as well as cutting the entry flap out so that this painstaking work can readily be seen.

When this work has been carried out satisfactorily, cement the completed cockpit interior into one half and join the two fuselage halves together. The detailing on the fuselage is rather heavy, so once the assembly has set, fill all the panel lines with body putty then sand off *all* the panel and rib detail. The

same treatment should also be applied to the wings and tailplanes, final sanding being with a very fine grade of wet and dry paper. If this work is done carefully it will still be possible to see the original lines which will show up as black strips on the plastic. Take some 30 thou plastic card and cut it into two and three inch lengths about 1/8 inch wide; stretch this in the same way as sprue and the result will be rectangular cross-sectioned strips. It is possible to use Microstrip for this but it is too wide as it comes and cutting it to thinner strips can be difficult.

Take the fuselage, and cut pieces of the stretched strip to the lengths of the rear fuselage stringers and bulkheads, then cement these in place with liquid cement. This part of the operation requires very careful application of the

The open cockpit, entry flap, rigging and fuselage detail from stretched sprue can be seen in this shot of the modified Sea Gladiator.

The Gladiator under construction. Extra fuselage rib detail and the scratch-built seat leaning against the port tailplane can be seen.

The original Blenheim cowling on the left, with the new cowling modified from it, engine and propeller.

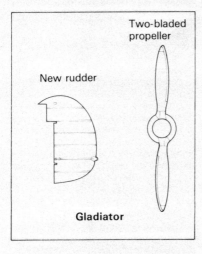

Two-bladed propeller

New rudder

Gladiator

adhesive; tube cement will *not* do for this work and it is stressed that Mekpak or Humbrol liquid cement must be used. Apply the cement with a fine brush, at the same time making sure that the stretched card is in the correct position. Liquid cement might cause a slight 'crazing' to occur between the stringers but don't worry about this as it faithfully reproduces the doped fabric covering of the rear fuselage and looks very effective when it is painted. The same work is carried out on the wings, tailplane and rudder, following the lines which were previously moulded into the surfaces. It is rather tedious and demanding and special care must be taken not to get a doped fabric effect on the forward cowlings, which were metal. The end result more than repays

the patience needed for once the card strips are dry and lightly sanded they really do make the Gladiator look as though it is a fabric-covered machine.

The machine-guns in the fuselage and wing blisters should be removed and replaced with new ones made from stretched sprue or plastic rod.

One important characteristic of the Gladiator, which is not captured by the kit, is the engine cowling. This is rectified by using a cowling from the Airfix Blenheim IV kit, which is modified by having a section cut off the rear so that the total width is 13/32 inch. The small intake on the under surface of the cowling needs slight reshaping before fitting, and if an early two-bladed version is being modelled this must be omitted completely. Exhaust pipes are made from stretched sprue, although those in the kit can be used if time is spent on improving their general shape.

The two-bladed propeller in the kit must be completely reworked if it is to be used at all, but by the time World War 2 started all Gladiators in squadron service had the three-bladed propeller so this must be fitted to any model which depicts an aircraft of this period.

The propeller, which is 1¾ inches in diameter, must either be made from plastic card or obtained from the spares box. The spinner shown on the drawings was not always fitted, but photographs of the Malta Gladiators usually show it, so if this model is chosen one must be fabricated. On my model I used a spinner from a Revell Spitfire suitably reduced in overall size.

The three Gladiators used in Malta were, in fact, Sea Gladiators, so to be strictly accurate an arrestor hook should be fitted under the rear fuselage, but there is photographic evidence which seems to indicate that at least one of these aircraft had this removed during its time in Malta.

Once all the work has been carried out the kit components should be assembled in the order shown in the instructions, but for ease in fitting the upper wing, glue the interplane struts — which, incidentally, can be greatly improved by sanding them to a more convincing aerofoil section — in place

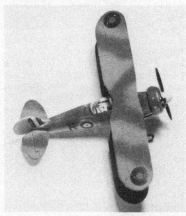

Two more views of the completed Sea Gladiator model.

and allow them to nearly set. Place the wing on the fuselage, which should by now have the lower wing fitted, and match the struts into their locating holes. Now gently remove the assembly and allow the struts to set hard before finally offering them up to the lower wing and cementing them firmly in place. The cabane struts are located in exactly the same way and should automatically fall into place when the top wing is finally fixed.

Cockpit interior is painted a light apple green colour and the engine matt black highlighted with silver or steel paint dry-brushed across the cylinders.

As mentioned earlier a wide variety of finishes are possible with this model and plenty of reference can be found in Profile No 98, *Camouflage and Marking* No 5, Hylton Lacey's *British Fighters of WW 2* Vol 1 and Aircam/ Airwar No 1. The latter shows a particularly attractive scheme for a Gladiator finished with the split black/ white under surfaces. The Malta Sea Gladiators were Dark Slate Grey and Ocean Grey camouflage on the top surfaces, and Sky Type S underneath. Markings are available from a variety of

sources and the rub-down type produced by Blick on sheets M9, M10 and M16 are particularly useful, not only for this model but others of the World War 2 period.

Once all markings have been applied the model should be rigged with either stretched sprue or 44 swg enamel wire held in place by PVA white household glue, which is useful as it dries to a transparent finish.

The Malta aircraft were very badly weathered, so if you are modelling one of these as it appeared in the campaign, it is best to apply this type of finish.

three

Hawker Hurricane

No collection of World War 2 fighters would be complete without at least one version of the Hawker Hurricane which, like its famous contemporary the Spitfire, will always have a place in aviation history. There are two kits of this aircraft available in the Airfix range, the earliest release being a Mk IV and the later being a Mk I or IIB. There are shortcomings on both kits but by combining parts from each of them acceptable models of various versions can be produced. Obviously the newer kit, which was released in 1972, is the better as far as fidelity of moulding and detail is concerned, but there are certain anomalies which do make it difficult to positively identify it as a Mk I.

One major problem is that the fuselage appears to be too shallow behind the cockpit, which itself is not

Hurricane 1 of 85 Squadron.

deep enough. This can be rectified by cementing a strip of plastic card along the top of the fuselage behind the cockpit, fairing this in with body putty, then sanding the additional parts into the contours of the fuselage. This adds the extra touch of depth but it also means that a new canopy must be made, although the one from the earlier kit is just about right and will fit with a little trimming. The other problem is a little more difficult to rectify as it concerns the overall length of the nose. The Mk II and later versions had an additional seven inches added to the nose which gave them a much more rangy look, but to add this amount in 1:72 scale is difficult unless you are well practised and a stickler for 100 per cent accuracy, which is a high standard to aim for anyway on a mass-produced commercial kit. As it is, the fuselage looks about right for a Mk I, but this version is also let down a trifle by the short blunt spinner provided for it. This, however, can be rectified by slightly reducing its rear diameter and generally cleaning up the shape. The other spinner in the kit is the long pointed one associated with the Rotol propeller and is very good for later mark aircraft.

There are similar problems connected with the surface detailing for the Mk IIB and IV which had different armament access panels. The only way to solve these problems is to study photographs of the aircraft you have chosen to model, remove all the kit detail by careful sanding, then re-scribe

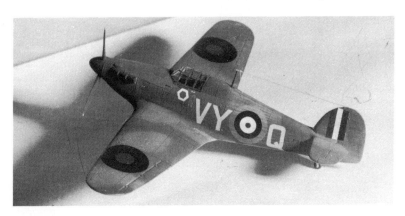

what you want. Early Mk I Hurricanes also had fabric-covered outer wing panels so again great caution must be exercised if a model with this feature is chosen. Whilst on the subject of minor changes which are aimed at obtaining as much authenticity as possible, it is also as well to mention that the oil splasher ring moulded around the nose was fitted to later versions of the Hurricane but not on the Mk I with the rounded spinner, so if you are using this make sure that the ring is sanded off before assembly is completed.

Finally, before getting down to one or two specific examples, the model is marred by huge 'Clydeside' style rivets which should be sanded off or at least reduced (if you happen to like rivet details on your models), irrespective of the version you choose to make.

Unlike the Spitfire, which was developed through various marks until the later versions bore little resemblance to the original, the Hurricane retained the same essential configuration through very few basic design changes and mark numbers. Most of these changes were confined to internal equipment, armament and engines, so the original outline was not appreciably altered, except by way of panel lines, etc, which have already been mentioned. This would therefore appear to limit the possibilities open to those who wish to add some conversions to their collections, but in fact is not so, as there are many minor variations which can be accomplished

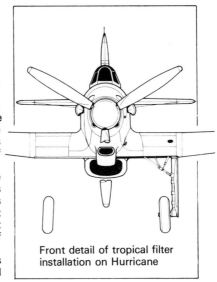

Front detail of tropical filter installation on Hurricane

with a minimum of effort. Such conversions as the prototype and the slip-wing Hurricane are interesting projects but do not fall into the general scope of this book which is mainly concerned with operational fighters or their derivatives. The following four examples form the basis on which others can be produced and include two photographic reconnaissance versions, which, although strictly speaking are not fighters, were essential to the RAF and can be included on an equal status in fighter collections.

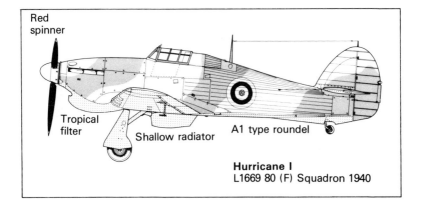

Red spinner

Tropical filter

Shallow radiator

A1 type roundel

Hurricane I
L1669 80 (F) Squadron 1940

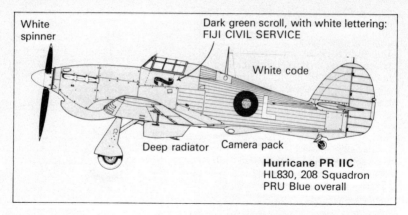

White spinner

Dark green scroll, with white lettering: FIJI CIVIL SERVICE

White code

Deep radiator   Camera pack

Hurricane PR IIC
HL830, 208 Squadron
PRU Blue overall

Mk I Tropical

This model requires only the addition of the Vokes tropical filter to the nose plus a change to the shorter exhaust stubs that were fitted to all Mk I Hurricanes. These exhausts should also be fitted if the kit version of the Battle of Britain Hurricane is being made, as those supplied in the kit are for later marks.

The tropical filter is built on the model by adding two layers of 20 thou plastic card to the underside of the nose, the bottom layer being slightly longer than the top one to produce the intake lip. When the two strips of card have set, build up the basic shape with filler and when this has set hard sand it to shape using progressively lighter grades of sandpaper. Use the short spinner from the kit and finish the model in a Sand/Dark Earth camouflage with a red spinner and Sky under surfaces. The aircraft drawn is L1669 as operated by No 80(F) Squadron whose spear and bell marking came from Blick Sheet M12, which also provides other

These views of the model Hurricane PR IIC of 208 Squadron clearly show the tropical filter and camera pack detail. See drawings for colour scheme details.

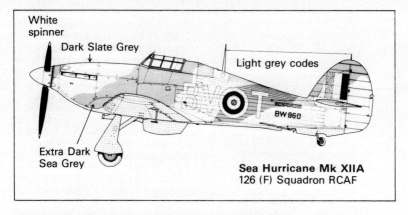

White spinner

Dark Slate Grey

Light grey codes

Extra Dark Sea Grey

Sea Hurricane Mk XIIA
126 (F) Squadron RCAF

BM·T
BW860

individual markings for fighter and bomber aircraft of World War 2. As with all examples in this book there are many alternative schemes to be found in publications such as Profiles, *Camouflage and Markings* and Michael Bowyer's *Fighting Colours* (published by PSL) which no self-respecting modeller of World War 2 fighters should be without.

Mk I PR

The aircraft chosen for this conversion had a camera pack carrying three 14-inch cameras under the rear fuselage just aft of the centre-section. This housing was built in exactly the same way as the tropical filter, although on this occasion three layers of plastic card were used. If an aircraft of this type was used in the tropics it

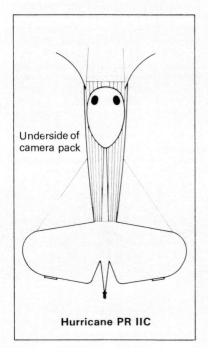

Underside of camera pack

Hurricane PR IIC

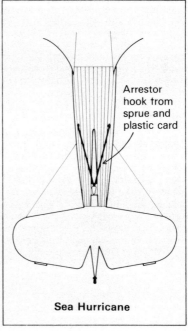

Arrestor hook from sprue and plastic card

Sea Hurricane

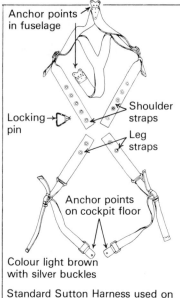

Anchor points
in fuselage

Locking →
pin

Shoulder
straps

Leg
straps

Anchor points
on cockpit floor

Colour light brown
with silver buckles

Standard Sutton Harness used on
several British World War 2 fighters
including the Spitfire and Hurricane

was also fitted with the tropical filter as
described above when it became
classified as the Mk I PR(Trop). In
either case, the longer spinner is used
and all armament deleted. Finish was
usually light blue overall with 'B' type
roundels on the wing top surfaces and
fuselage, the under surfaces being
unmarked.

Mk PR IIC

This aircraft should be built as the Mk
IV using the longer exhaust stubs and a
tropical filter added as for the Mk I
(Trop). However, this aircraft, like all
Mk IIs and IVs, had a slightly deeper
radiator intake under the wing centre-
section. The kit radiator is deepened by
adding a lamination of 10 thou plastic
card to the underside and fairing this in
with filler before sanding to the desired

contours. The camera bay is made in
exactly the same way as described for
the Mk I PR but is a different shape,
being more rounded at the front.

No armament is fitted and the Rotol
propeller with longer spinner is used. A
typical finish would be PRU Blue overall
with 'B' type roundels on fuselage and
wing top surfaces but no markings
underneath. In many cases the fin flash
was not carried. The example illustrated is from No 208 Squadron and has
a white spinner and individual aircraft
letter in the same colour.

The Royal Navy operated the
Hurricane in various guises, one of
which was the Mk IC which used a
Merlin III engine but had the cannon-
armed wing associated with the
Mk IIC. The earliest versions had an
arrestor hook added to the rear
fuselage but this was later modified in
design and catapult spools were also
fitted. Apart from the addition of the
arrestor hook, the Sea Hurricanes only
differed in the equipment, such as
radios and armament, with which they
were fitted.

The Sea Hurricane IA was basically a
standard eight-gunned Mk I adapted
for operations from catapults on armed
merchant ships (CAM-ships). The Sea
Hurricane Mk IB was fitted with
arrestor gear and catapult spools, and
this was followed by the Sea Hurricane
Mk IC which had the four-cannon
wing. The final version was the Sea
Hurricane Mk IIC with the four-cannon
wing and Merlin XX engine. The
drawing shows the basic arrestor hook
installation for early versions, although
there was little difference between
those fitted to all Sea Hurricanes.

Cockpit interior colours for both RAF
and RN Hurricanes was light apple
green, with black instrument panels
having light green luminous figures and
needles. The Sutton-type safety harness was a lightish green/brown with
black stitching and silver buckles.

four

Spitfires and Seafires

The Supermarine Spitfire is probably the most famous fighter aircraft ever produced. Even today, 40 years after its first flight, practically every schoolboy knows of its exploits and will readily call it to mind if asked to name a fighter aircraft. Produced in quantities which were second only to its equally famous opponent the Bf 109, over 25 variations went into major production and it continued to serve with the RAF long after the end of World War 2. It is not surprising therefore that every major manufacturer of plastic construction kits has produced at least one version of this important aircraft; sometimes duplicating each other's efforts, but occasionally producing a version with which their competitors have not bothered. By combining parts from all available 1:72 scale kits, it is possible to produce a tremendous number of marks and variations. It would be possible fill several books the length of this Guide confined solely to the Spitfire, so the task in condensing just a few examples into the following pages is a major undertaking fraught with danger.

Many of the tips given can be used on any version of the Spitfire, and no doubt other modellers will disagree with my conclusions, or offer better alternatives. Finding out for oneself is one of the joys of modelling, and there has been so much material published about the Spitfire that there really are no excuses for anyone who so wishes to make a definitive study of the aircraft then produce models in line with what he might discover. To the serious modeller I heartily recommend a private publication by American modeller John R. Beaman titled *Calling all Spitfires*. This and its update both contain everything there is to know about available kits and necessary modifications to them, as well as conversion possibilities. John has kindly allowed me to draw on his publications for parts of this section, which because of necessity is very brief, but a note to him at 2512 Overbrook Drive, Greensboro, NC 27408, USA, will bring full details of the mentioned books and open a complete new modelling vista for those who are Spitfire-orientated.

Airfix have produced three 1:72 scale kits of this aircraft: the first was one of their very first and is no longer available; the second is now very old and, compared with later releases of the same aircraft (a Mk IX) by other

Weathering on the wing roots and tailplanes of a Spitfire Mk Vc. This has been done by applying 'rub and buff', covering the areas with masking tape, overspraying then removing the masking fluid.

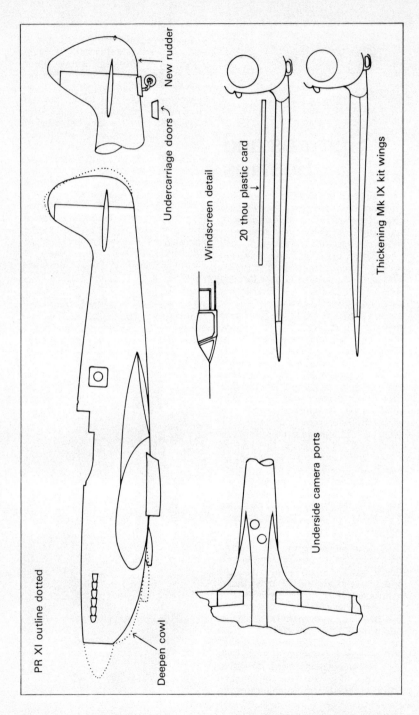

New rudder

Undercarriage doors

PR XI outline dotted

Deepen cowl

Windscreen detail

20 thou plastic card

Thickening Mk IX kit wings

Underside camera ports

Modelling World War 2 Fighters

manufacturers, is suspect in accuracy; but the third, which is a Mk Vb, is probably the best kit of the Spitfire available anywhere.

As the Mk IX and Mk Vb are inexpensive and readily available, they are the ones chosen for the conversions which follow. It is advisable to purchase both the Frog and Matchbox Spitfires which are, in the case of the former, a Mk Ia, Mk XIV and a Mk VIII/IX, and in the latter a Mk IX, as these yield many useful parts. It is not money wasted or a method of spending a lot to produce one good model, as all the pieces left over can be used in other conversions which are almost certain to follow, since it is very rare that one version will satisfy the ardent modeller. My own collection runs to nine models which I have every intention of adding to when time permits.

There seems to be little point in detailing how to convert the Airfix Mk Vb back to an early Mk Ia or II, as there are available good kits of this version, but many of the detailing points made in the models described can be used whichever model is being constructed.

Spitfire PR Mk XI

Nomenclature associated with the Spitfire becomes very confusing as there were many different wing plan-forms and armament variations, some of which are shown on the accompanying drawings. It would only serve to confuse the reader if an explanation was attempted, so it is strongly recommended that the subject matter chosen is studied most carefully before work is carried out on any model. In addition to suffix letters to mark numbers, such as Mk IXc or Mk IXe, in these cases the letter referring to the type of wing fitted, there were also prefix letters such as FR or PR. The FR was a 'Fighter Reconnaissance' aircraft fitted with some armament, whereas the PR was an unarmed 'Photographic Reconnaissance' machine.

The basic kit for this conversion is the Airfix Mk IX which is correct in overall length but is not deep enough under the front cowling. It can also be improved by the fitting of wheels from the later Mk V or the Frog Mk I/II, the latter having a particularly good tailwheel. The Mk IXc, which is the model depicted by the kit, can also be converted to a Mk IXe by the same change of wing armament detailed in the next conversion, and the more pointed rudder as supplied in the Frog and Matchbox kits of this aircraft. But back to the PR XI, which was much the same as the PR X, the only difference being that the Mk X had a pressurised cockpit. Assemble the fuselage components after adding cockpit detail, then build up a deeper lower cowl line with body putty or laminations of plastic card. This deeper cowling accommodated a tank of greater oil capacity, which was not fitted to the Mk IX. The carburettor intake under the

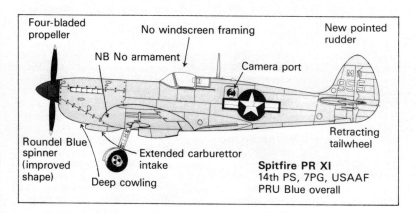

Four-bladed propeller

No windscreen framing

New pointed rudder

NB No armament

Camera port

Roundel Blue spinner (improved shape)

Extended carburettor intake

Deep cowling

Retracting tailwheel

Spitfire PR XI
14th PS, 7PG, USAAF
PRU Blue overall

Work in progress on the Spitfire PR Mk XI. The cannon blisters have been removed from—in this case—Matchbox wings, and the camera port added behind the cockpit. Filler has been applied to the wing roots, tailplanes and area where blisters have been removed.

wings must be cut off and a new longer one made from laminated card or a carved piece of sprue. This is cemented back on slightly forward of its original position.

The top decking forward of the cockpit needs to be slightly more rounded at the front end, just behind the spinner, which is also best replaced by the same component from the Matchbox kit. The Airfix four-bladed propeller is not strictly accurate so once again the Matchbox kit can be raided for this component. If you have decided that the luxury of two different kits is not for you then add putty to the spinner to improve its shape and make slightly wider blades from plastic card; both these operations are tricky and the original is not so far out to be too noticeable except by the few genuine Spitfire experts; so if you can live with the kit spinner and propeller, by all means do so.

Before turning to the wings, drill a hole 3/32 inch in diameter in the centre of the scribed radio hatch just aft of the

cockpit, and into this insert a piece of clear plastic sprue. This is cut off flush with the fuselage then sanded smooth and polished to represent the camera port. The cockpit canopy should be sanded with a light grade wet and dry paper, to remove all windscreen detail, then polished with toothpaste to restore its original transparency. The PR XI had a rounded windscreen with no frame as well as a blown canopy. The former is achieved as described but the latter can only be made by vac-forming a completely new canopy. Once again in 1:72 scale the blown effect would be very small so it might be worthwhile overlooking this minor area.

The major problem with the Airfix Mk IX wing is that it is too thin when viewed from the front. This can be rectified by sanding off all the top surface detail—the cannon bulges must be removed in any case for a PR version—then cementing a layer of 20 thou plastic card to the whole top wing area. When the card has set, taper it

Modelling World War 2 Fighters

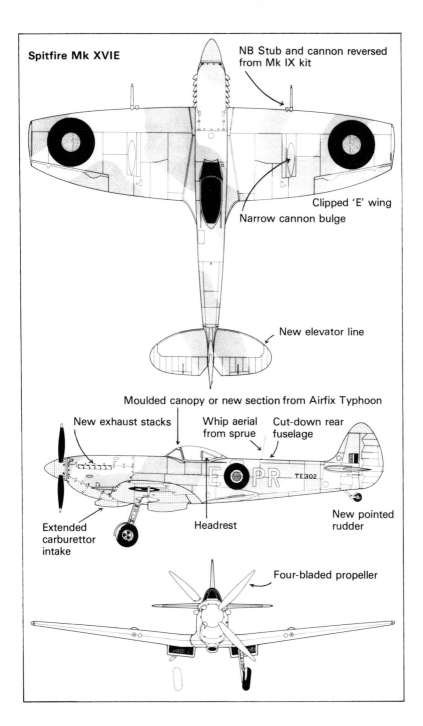

Spitfire Mk XVIE

NB Stub and cannon reversed from Mk IX kit

Clipped 'E' wing

Narrow cannon bulge

New elevator line

Moulded canopy or new section from Airfix Typhoon

New exhaust stacks

Whip aerial from sprue

Cut-down rear fuselage

Extended carburettor intake

Headrest

New pointed rudder

Four-bladed propeller

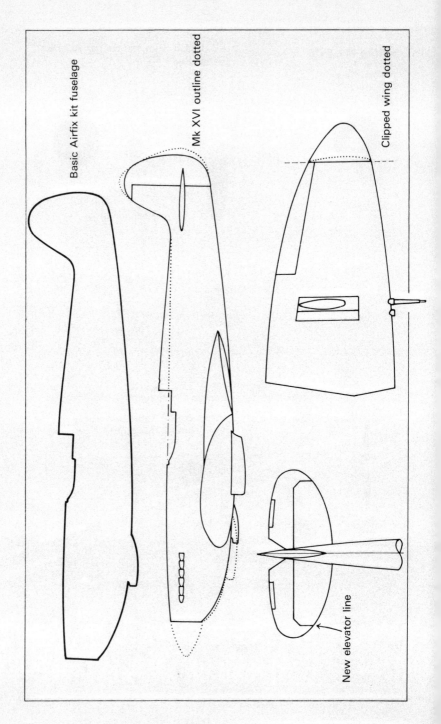

Basic Airfix kit fuselage

Mk XVI outline dotted

Clipped wing dotted

New elevator line

into the wingtips, trailing and leading edges by sanding and judicious use of filler. When this has been done, compare the wing top surface with the Mk V wing and it will be seen that there is a slight bulge above the main wheel housing. This should also appear on the Mk IX or PR XI and can be added with a small piece of plastic card faired in with filler. Just forward of this bulge there should be a peg which protrudes when the wheels are down, thus giving the pilot visual indication of his undercarriage position. This is added by drilling a very small hole and inserting a piece of stretched sprue to both wings. The peg is painted red on the completed model. This modification should be added to the Spitfire and Seafire conversions under discussion.

As already mentioned, the main gear is best replaced with that from the Frog kit if you want a better representation of the Spitfire undercarriage. A new pointed rudder can easily be made from plastic card and sanded to the correct aerofoil section, and should replace the rounded rudder moulded on the kit. Final attention can be given to the exhaust stacks, which should be narrower in plan view and are slightly too wide, as well as too far forward. If you don't want to remove these then they can be improved acceptably by

careful use of a sharp modelling knife in trimming them to a better shape. The appearance is further improved by scribing a line around the edges of the exhausts to give the impression they protrude through the cowling and are not moulded to it.

All PR Spitfires had a mirror attached to the top of the windscreen and this is made from a sliver of sprue and a small piece of paper or 5 thou plastic card. This component should be fitted after all other work, including painting, has been completed, otherwise it will continually be knocked off. A touch of Araldite, Devcon or PVA glue will not mar the canopy and will set quickly enough to prevent the necessity of holding the mirror in place for a long period until it has set.

There are so many published colour schemes for Spitfires readily available,

Two views of the Spitfire PR Mk XI in USAAF markings. The deeper chin line of the fuselage is visible in the side view.

Plan view of the Mk XVI Spitfire showing the clipped wings and re-arranged cannons.

that there is no point in making recommendations here. The examples illustrated are typical for the aircraft concerned.

The American-operated PR Mk XI is finished PRU Blue overall with white codes, all of which were obtained from the spares box.

Spitfire Mk XVIe

The Mk XVI Spitfire was identical to the Mk IX except for the fact that it was powered by a Packard-built Rolls-Royce Merlin engine. After an early production batch they were all built with a cut-down rear fuselage and a tear drop canopy; similarly some late production Mk IXes had the same modifications and there is no way of telling these apart except through identification of serial numbers. Most Mk XVIs had the 'e' wing with clipped tips, although the normal tip was also to be seen; it is also possible that some had the 'c' wing which can be identified by the narrower cannon bulge on the top surface. This conversion however, is based on the majority of this version which is with a clipped 'e' wing.

Start by cementing the two fuselage halves together and when they are set cut off the raised rear portion of the fuselage in a straight line from the lower edge of the cockpit to the front of the fin. Use a fretsaw or sharp modelling knife and try to keep the cuts on both halves parallel and to the same depth. The new lower line to the rear fuselage can be made from a piece of ¼ inch square hard balsa wood which is inserted into the fuselage and carved to shape, final finishing being with a very fine grade flour paper and grain filler. An alternative is to separate the section removed along the original top join line, and cement one piece back into the fuselage, building up to the right height and sealing the joins along the fuselage with filler, which is also then sanded to the correct profile. When this has been done, remove the rudder and fit a new pointed one as all Mk XVIs were equipped with this. The lower cowling must be corrected in shape, but remember it is not as deep as the one on the PR Mk XI. The top section of the cowling behind the propeller is also modified as for the previous conversion. Cockpit detail can be added at this stage and should include a raised headrest support, made from plastic card, behind the seat. The carburettor intake can be left as it is in the kit but tidied up with the front end hollowed out, or extended as for the PR Mk XI. Both types were used on the MK XVI, but few operational machines had the short intake, so it is advisable to fit the longer one as described for the PR Mk XI if you wish your model to represent a typical service aircraft.

The exhaust stacks and propeller need the same attention as the previous conversion, and it is also advisable to replace the tailwheel.

The wings present a problem because, as the cannon blister have to be retained, it is not so easy to make them thicker. There are two ways to do this. One is to remove the blister and add plastic card as before, then scratch-build a new blister; or, add plastic card to either side of the existing blister along the entire length of the wing and fair this into the correct profile. This method is the easiest as the making of new blisters, which must of course be identical, is a little tricky. The blisters themselves are a little too wide but it is easy to file or sand some of the unwanted plastic away on either side.

Another view of the Mk XVI showing the cut-down rear fuselage and new shaped fin/rudder.

The new blisters are centered on the new cannon position and not on the 'c' wing cannon centre-line. So if you do reshape them keep this in mind when material is being removed. The ideal solution is to use the narrow blisters from the Matchbox kit but this involves removing the complete panel from this and relocating it into a similar area in the Airfix wing, which would be more tricky than removing the original blisters and making new ones from plastic card or filler.

When this has been carried out, remove the cannons and the two stubs and make two new cannons from sprue. These are cemented back in place where the original stubs were, and new stubs—which can in fact be left when the cannons are removed— placed where the cannons were. In other words the positions of the cannons and stubs are reversed.

The wing tips are cut off at the tip just outboard of the line marked on the kit and the resulting blunt tips are sanded to a rounded section. The 'pip' type navigation lights on the original are replaced by painting lights at the forward tips of the clipped wings. The radiators under the wings benefit by having their lower edges slightly rounded and the internal finning represented by small pieces cut from a pair of lady's tights and cemented to plastic card inserts. This modification will improve any version of the Spitfire based on the kit in question.

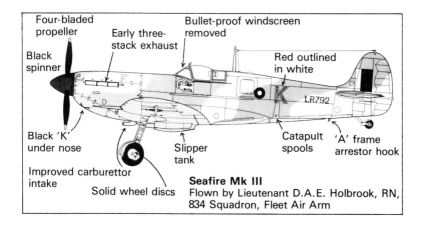

Four-bladed propeller

Early three-stack exhaust

Bullet-proof windscreen removed

Black spinner

Red outlined in white

Black 'K' under nose

Catapult spools

'A' frame arrestor hook

Improved carburettor intake

Slipper tank

Solid wheel discs

Seafire Mk III
Flown by Lieutenant D.A.E. Holbrook, RN, 834 Squadron, Fleet Air Arm

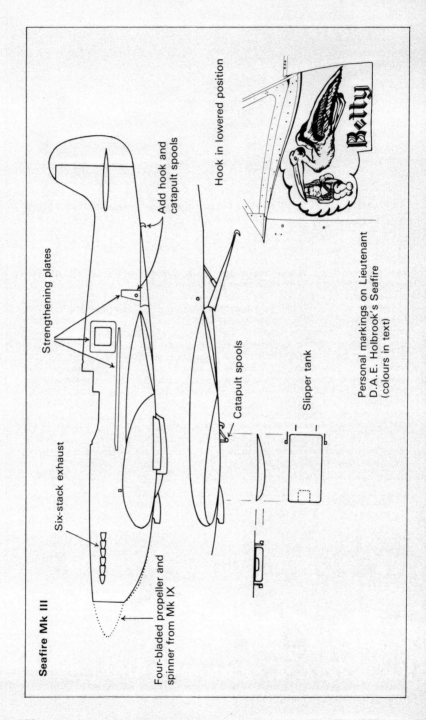

Seafire Mk III

Six-stack exhaust

Four-bladed propeller and spinner from Mk IX

Strengthening plates

Add hook and catapult spools

Hook in lowered position

Catapult spools

Slipper tank

Personal markings on Lieutenant D.A.E. Holbrook's Seafire (colours in text)

Betty

The tailplanes and elevators must now be sanded completely smooth and a new elevator hinge line scribed in as shown on the drawing. The most difficult part of this conversion is the cockpit canopy, the best method being to mould a new blister canopy using the proven male/female mould method, but there are alternatives. A canopy from the Airfix Typhoon is close, especially if the original Spitfire windscreen is retained and only the blown portion from the rear of the Typhoon's canopy is used. To complete the construction add a whip aerial from stretched sprue, new undercarriage doors from thin plastic card—again something from which all models benefit—and a new pitot head fashioned from sprue or Microstrip.

Spitfire MK XVIs were used post-war by the RAF and Auxiliary Air Force, so there are plenty of schemes available if you care to look for them.

Seafire III

From the beginning of the war the Fleet Air Arm soldiered on with fighters which were outclassed by their opponents, so it is not surprising that they looked rather enviously at the more modern equipment of the RAF, especially the Spitfire. Eventually this aircraft went to sea as the Seafire Mk I, II or III, all of which were based on the Spitfire V so have the shorter fuselage

associated with this mark rather than the longer one of the Mk IX.

The Seafire I was basically a Spitfire Vb with an arrestor hook, some of which were also fitted with the large Vokes-type tropical filter, but in the interests of performances these were often removed.

The Seafire IIc was a Spitfire Vc using the Universal type 'c' wing. These were all built as Seafires whereas the Seafire Ibs were all converted from Spitfires. One of the many problems encountered with the seagoing Spitfire was the lack of wing folding, but this was rectified on the Seafire III which used a 'c' wing modified to fold in two places: outboard of the main gear, and at the tips. Folding had to be carried out manually and the hinging mechanism did result in a marginal loss of performance.

The Seafire III used the uprated Merlin of the Mk IX Spitfire but this was installed in the Mk V airframe and did not result in a longer fuselage length. Construction of this version is simple but careful attention must be paid to detail. The kit used is the Airfix Mk Vb and construction is commenced exactly as laid down in the kit instructions. When the fuselage has been assembled, cement strengthening strips from the rear of the fuel tank bay to the bulkhead behind the radio hatch.

Seafire IIc and IIIcs of 834 Squadron Fleet Air Arm in Ceylon in 1944. Finish is Sky Type S under surfaces with Dark Sea Grey and Slate Grey camouflage on top surfaces. Codes are red outlined in white and serials are black. Small SEAC roundels are carried in all positions. Fin flash is white and dark blue (D.A.E. Holbrook).

The personal marking of Lieutenant D.A.E. Holbrook on Seafire IIIc LR792 'K'. This is the aircraft featured in the drawings and model. Background is pale blue, stork is white with black detail, baby is pink, name 'Betty' is black. This insignia was painted on Lieutenant Holbrook's Seafire by his ground crew after the W/T office received a 'cable' advising him of the birth of his son Martin, the artist who has illustrated this book. It was painted overnight whilst the pilot was celebrating his news in the time-honoured tradition of the Senior Service. . .

These are clearly shown on the drawing and are made from 5 thou plastic card attached with liquid cement. These strips reinforced the main fuselage longerons and helped them take the additional strain of deck landings and catapult launches. Similar strengthening was carried out around the radio hatch, and again plastic card is used to reproduce this. These strips must be sanded down when they are dry until they are barely perceptible, as in 1:72 scale they are very small and can hardly be seen. An alternative to plastic card is thin writing paper which requires no sanding, but unless it is treated to a coat of matt varnish before painting, will not absorb the final coat in a way that looks authentic. The very thin plastic card supplied in the Airfix 54 mm figure kits is ideal for this work if you want to avoid the sanding down of the more easily obtained thicker material.

On the Seafire an 'A' frame arrestor hook was fitted under the rear fuselage, inside a triangular-shaped panel which was lowered from just behind the wing roots. When the hook is retracted all that can be seen is the hooked end just forward of the tail wheel, but close examination of photographs often shows a line where the fairing retracts. To simulate this, use very fine stretched sprue fixed with liquid cement to mark the outline of the fairing, and thick flat sprue, curved into a hook shape whilst it is still warm, for the hook. When it is dry sand the sprue very carefully until it is just a sliver; when painted this looks most authentic and In my opinion is better than a scribed line.

Early Seafire IIIs were fitted with the three fishtail exhaust as supplied in the Vb kit, but the L III used the six-stack exhaust as the Mk IX. Both versions used a four-bladed propeller so this must be taken from either the Airfix Mk IX, suitably modified, or better still the Matchbox kit of the same aircraft. Unless you want to scratch-build the six-stack exhaust, this must also be taken from the Matchbox kit and trimmed to fit the recess in the Mk Vb fuselage. The Seafire drawn is one flown by Lieutenant D.A.E. Holbrook RN, whilst he was with No 834 Squadron, and is shown with the six-stack exhaust. However, photographs in this pilot's collection show that the aircraft did have the three fishtail exhaust stacks at one time in its life.

Final work on the fuselage involves removal of the thick bulletproof windscreen as moulded in the Vb kit. This was fitted internally on the Seafire III and if you are a masochist you can attempt to place it inside the screen! To remove the thick screen use a flat file in even strokes, making sure that it is kept flat, then complete the work with fine grade wet and dry, and restore clarity by polishing with toothpaste.

Standardisation of the 'c' wing armament on the Seafire III, as well as a change from drum to belt-fed ammunition for the wing cannons, means that some modification has to be carried out to the Spitfire kit wings. The stub outboard of the cannons on the 'c' wing was completely deleted from the Seafire III and late Mk IIc, but as the

Modelling World War 2 Fighters

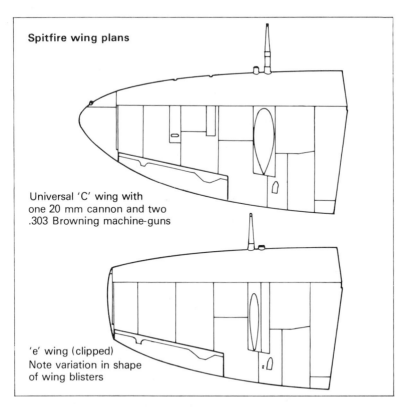

Spitfire wing plans

Universal 'C' wing with
one 20 mm cannon and two
.303 Browning machine-guns

'e' wing (clipped)
Note variation in shape
of wing blisters

wing in the kit is a 'b' it does not present
any problems as this did not have the
stub in any case. On the Seafire IIc the
stub was removed and the hole faired in
with a metal plate which was often left
in its natural state, so a drop of silver
paint will represent this if a IIc is being
built.

For the IIIc the large bulge on the
wing top surface must be completely
removed as it is not only too wide but
also in the wrong position, being much
further back on the Seafire. The ideal

*A Seafire IIc of 834 Squadron after a
landing accident aboard a carrier. The
aluminium plate over the outboard
cannon stub is clearly visible. The
object hanging from the cockpit is the
pilot's helmet. Note the small slim
cannon blisters on the wing top
surfaces* (D.A.E. Holbrook).

Three views of the model Seafire IIIc LR792 'K'. The side view clearly shows the arrestor hook and flat windscreen as well as the solid discs to the main wheels.

solution is to use the top surfaces from the Matchbox kit, which by now has been robbed of its propeller, spinner and exhaust stacks anyway. These will need some trimming to fit the Airfix wing and filler will have to be applied at the root, but it does match up quite well and the effort is worthwhile. The alternative is to sand off the Airfix blisters and make new ones from plastic card or filler. The underwing blister is also too big and too far forward so this must be removed and replaced by a scratch-built pair, or alternatively the whole of the Match-

box wing could be used. This saves a lot of work in changing the larger Airfix blisters, but creates additional work in matching the various components. The choice is yours!

The under surfaces of the Airfix wing need some attention from filler, this being used to fill the two triangular-shaped holes by the wheel wells. These are, in fact, panels on the actual aircraft but as moulded by Airfix appear to have the covers left off, so it is best to fill them completely and sand smooth. The ejector slot for spent links from the cannons is not shown and should be scribed in level with the wheel well and aft of the cannon barrel. The hole on the centre-line is the aircraft's down-ward identification light. It is marginally oversize but best left alone.

The carburettor intake is as the kit but can be improved by hollowing out the front end. The longer intake was fitted to the L III, which was a version powered by a low-rated Merlin engine. All of these, apart from the first few, were fitted with the six-stack exhaust, so in photographs they look very much like a Mk IX Spitfire.

Drill out the outboard machine-gun ports to make them look more convincing and replace the cannons with new ones shaped from sprue or hollow tube. Catapult spools were fitted to both sides of the fuselage aft of the wing roots and above the arrestor gear fairing; these are simply two small pieces of round sprue inserted into drilled holes. It was rare to see a Seafire III without a 60 or 90 gallon slipper tank

Modelling World War 2 Fighters

so this should be added and a good source, unless you want to build one from scratch, is the Frog Mk VIII/IX kit.

The model illustrated has very small SEAC roundels which came from an unidentified kit (those in the Frog Mk VIII/IX are too big) and the red code outlined in white was from a Letraset sheet. The personal insignia painted below the cockpit was a white and black stork on a blue cloud, the baby was pink, the bird's beak yellow and the name 'Betty' in black. Once again final choice of finish rests with the individual and there are many to choose from. After painting, add a round mirror to the top of the windscreen in the same way as was done for the PR Spitfire. In passing it is worth mentioning that most Seafires had solid discs, painted in the underside colour, over the cast wheel hubs, so if you choose to depict your model with this modification use the wheels from the Matchbox kit rather than those in the Airfix Vb.

Although the Seafire was greatly liked by its pilots, it proved to be rather delicate for the rigours of shipboard use and its undercarriage was particularly susceptible. Nonetheless, it performed legion service and makes an interesting modelling subject.

The foregoing conversions have only scratched the surface of possible Spitfire/Seafire variants, and remember that many of the details given can be used in any type of conversion, not only of the aircraft dealt with but many others as well.

five

Messerschmitt Bf 109

The Messerschmitt Bf 109 was produced in greater quantities than any other combat aircraft—apart from the Russian Il-2—and served with the Luftwaffe from the first to the last day of World War 2. It is equally as famous as its rival, the Spitfire, and was produced in as many different forms and variants. The main versions were identified by letters added to the type number, but within each type there was also a bewildering system of sub-types designated by suffix codes defining armament and airframe changes. *Airfix Magazine Guide* No 23 outlines the main Bf 109 service types and is a good primer for those who wish to make a detailed study of Luftwaffe fighters.

Kits of the Bf 109 are almost as plentiful as those of the Spitfire and therefore enable a wide collection to be accumulated without the necessity of attempting too many difficult conversions. In view of this it would be pointless and space consuming to consider modifying the available Airfix kits, which are of the Bf 109E-4 and the Me 109G-6, but these two do enable the modeller to add other versions to his collection without too much effort, and serve to illustrate the German approach to various problems encountered in operations.

The older Airfix kit is of the Me 109G which, incidentally, was the type produced in the greatest quantity, and is basically a good kit although it needs correction in certain areas. These corrections are covered in *Airfix Magazine Guide* No 2 so will not be repeated here.

The increasing effectiveness of Allied high-altitude reconnaissance flights, plus the gradual move to higher combat altitudes, forced the Luftwaffe to seek a suitable deterrent in the form of an effective fighter which could meet the double threat on equal terms. Since the Bf 109 had been used in almost every role, it was natural that Messerschmitt's ubiquitous fighter should be considered a sound basis from which a design study should start.

Based on the Bf 109F, but with a considerably increased combat ceiling, the Bf 109H was put forward in early 1943 as a suitable interim measure. The idea was that, if this design proved the right formula, the aircraft could start to equip units whilst a much improved version was developed for entry into service by the end of 1944.

The Bf 109H was originally conceived with a standard Bf 109F

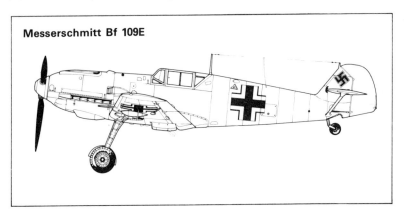

Messerschmitt Bf 109E

Modelling World War 2 Fighters

The standard Airfix Bf 109G with a K in the background.

airframe, an increased wingspan of just over 39 feet, and an uprated DB 601 engine. A number of pre-production aircraft using standard Bf 109F fuselages and designated Bf 109H-O, together with a few Bf 109H-1s—which was basically the same aircraft but with slight equipment changes—were built and used for service evaluation at Guyancourt, near Paris, during 1944. But although various models using different power plants and Me 109G variant airframes, and a new design called the Me 209-11, were developed in parallel, they were all too late to see service and, like so many promising Luftwaffe design requirements, came to untimely ends with the final collapse of Germany. However, unlike some interim designs, the Bf 109H did actually see limited service and is an interesting conversion that will yield a further variant of this famous fighter.

Bf 109H

Two Airfix kits of the Me 109G are required but the parts not used from the second kit make useful additions to the spares box, especially if it is intended to add more 109s to a miniature Luftwaffe.

The conversion is started by assembling Parts 4, 5, 6 and 7 as shown in the kit instructions, first adding any detail to the cockpit area and omitting Parts 1, 2 and 3—the propeller and spinner assembly. When the fuselage is dry, remove the two cannon breech block covers to convert the basic shape to the

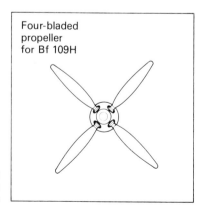

Four-bladed propeller for Bf 109H

Messerschmitt Bf 109

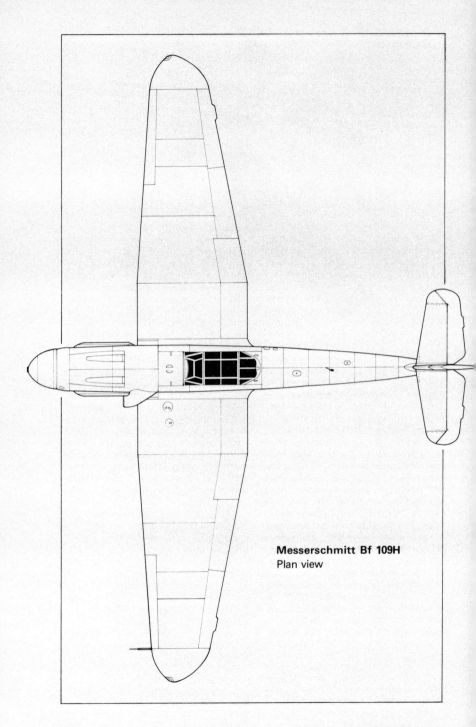

Messerschmitt Bf 109H
Plan view

Modelling World War 2 Fighters

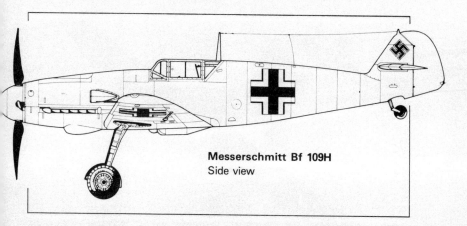

Messerschmitt Bf 109H
Side view

Bf 109F fuselage. These can be removed successfully with a sharp modelling knife which should be used to reduce the rounded shapes to flat discs, and then a fairly coarse grade of wet and dry to sand the flats into the fuselage contours. Do not try to remove all the bulge with the knife as there is a danger of taking too much off, then having to use filler to hide the resulting hole. Finish the surgery with a fine grade wet and dry paper, at the same time removing all traces of join lines, etc.

Next remove the rudder along the hinge line and the location point under the centre-section where the long range belly tank or bomb is fitted on the kit version. The Bf 109H used the taller, more rounded-tipped rudder associated with the late 'G' version, so a new one is made from plastic card or balsa using the pattern shown on the drawing. Two laminations of 30 thou plastic card are probably the best material for this small component, which should be attached to the stern post of the fin and sanded to an aerofoil section. The 'H' also had wider chord and longer span tailplanes and these are also made from plastic card sanded to an aerofoil section with the elevator hinge line scribed in. When the new tailplanes are fitted to the fuselage it will be noticed that their leading edge is in line with the leading edge of the fin, which results in some filler being required between the root of the

tailplanes and the curvature of the fin. This should be carried out with great care and the filler left to dry really hard before any attempt is made at sanding it to shape. The increased span of the tailplane resulted in the re-introduction of bracing struts as used on the Bf 109E. These are made from stretched sprue or the barrels of the underwing cannons, Parts 23 and 24, but should not be attached at this stage or they will easily be removed during final finishing prior to painting.

The wingspan of the 'H' was increased by 6 feet 6 inches on the actual aircraft, which means that a 1 3/32-inch section has to be added to the model. This was a parallel chord centre-section carrying two radiators and resulted in a much increased undercarriage track.

Take one complete set of wings from the second kit, Parts 8, 9, 10 and 11, and assemble them as shown in the kit instructions. At the same time the set from the original kit should also be put together in the same way. Select the wings that are to be used for the new centre-section and put the others well out of the way as it becomes easy to get them mixed up and find that when the work has been completed two port or starboard wings have been made instead of a pair!

Measure 9/16-inch from the wing root and cut off the remaining wing area. Do this to both wings, making sure that the cut lines are parallel and

Messerschmitt Bf 109

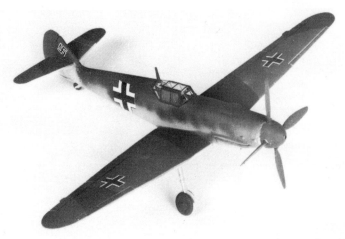

A Bf 109H converted from the Airfix kit. Note the increased span, four-bladed propeller and new braced tailplane.

the cut edge is cleaned and smoothed with sandpaper or wet and dry. When this work has been completed satisfactorily, cement the shortened wings to the fuselage. Now take the other complete wings and remove the radiators. This work will result in a considerable amount of filling being required, but do not do it at this stage. Cement the wings to the two roots attached to the fuselage, making sure that the dihederal is constant from the fuselage wing root to the tip. The locating tongue will fit into the section remaining on the root attached to the fuselage but there may be a small gap remaining on the top or bottom where the joint has been made. When this assembly is dry, work can start on filling and adding plastic card where necessary. It will be seen that a small triangle of plastic card is needed at the trailing

The increased span of the Bf 109H can be seen in this photograph which also shows another conversion, this time to the two-seat trainer. Both models were converted from the Airfix Me 109G kit.

Modelling World War 2 Fighters

edge of the centre-section to make this parallel to the leading edge, and this should be added at this time. Fill the join lines and the remains of the inner centre-section wheel wells, not forgetting any blemishes where the radiators were removed. Leave overnight to set, then carefully smooth with progressively lighter grades of glass-paper or wet and dry until a perfectly smooth surface is achieved. Score new flap lines on top and bottom of the centre-section, and give the whole model a coat of matt white or grey paint, which will not only help to show up any areas that need further work, but also give depth to the final colours.

The Bf 109H had a four-bladed airscrew which is made by taking the kit spinner, filling it with body putty to get rid of the original three location points for the three-bladed propeller, then drilling four new location points at 90° intervals. The propeller blades were broader than those on the Me 109G so will have to be found in the scrap box or scratch-built from plastic card. I used the blades from a P-51 suitably cut down in diameter and reshaped, but if no blades can be found and scratch-building is not your particular forté, use the ones from the two kits. These will not, of course, be strictly accurate.

Complete the model by adding the cockpit canopy, the shorter intake, Part 18, and the tailplane bracing struts. The streamlined blisters for these can be made with a small 'blob' of body putty added to their bases where they join the fuselage, suitably shaped when dry. Aileron balances can be made from stretched sprue and body putty or taken from the Frog Bf 109F kit if a spare one is available. The complete undercarriage is as per the kit, as is the aerial post.

Unfortunately, colour schemes for the Bf 109H are very hard to come by but photographs appear to indicate that it was finished in the standard Luftwaffe scheme of light blue under surfaces merging into light grey fuselage sides with light green mottle merging into dark green on the top, and dark green/light green splinter pattern on the wings. Transfers from the kit can be used but so far I have not been able to find any codes or unit markings applicable to this aircraft.

The high-flying Bf 109H makes an interesting talking point among modellers, especially if it is displayed alongside a standard aircraft, when its greatly increased wingspan becomes very evident indeed.

Bf 109T

The Bf 109E was the aircraft used extensively in the Battle of Britain and one which was somewhat neglected by the kit manufacturers until 1976 and early 1977. Prior to this only Revell produced a 1:72 scale kit, although in the very early days of the plastic model Airfix did, in fact, market a rather poor 109 which could, at a stretch of the

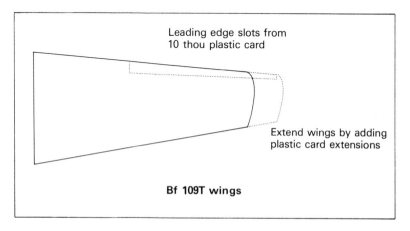

Leading edge slots from 10 thou plastic card

Extend wings by adding plastic card extensions

Bf 109T wings

Messerschmitt Bf 109

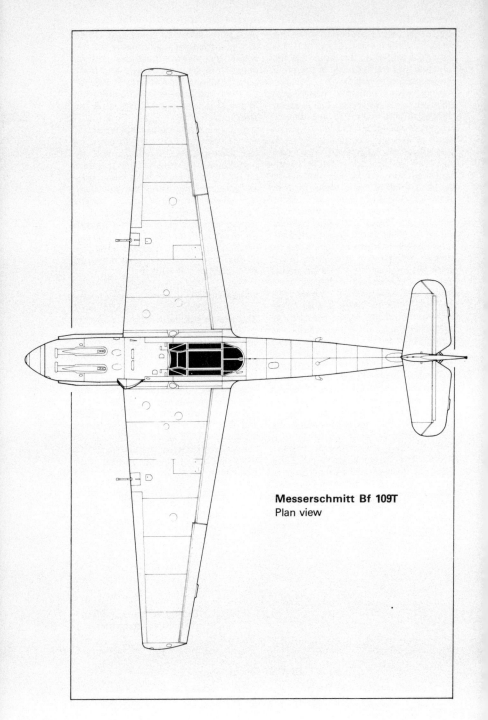

Messerschmitt Bf 109T
Plan view

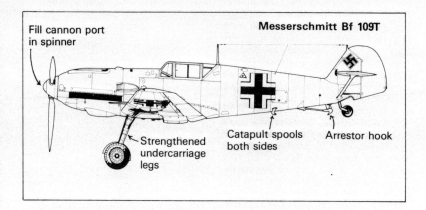

Fill cannon port in spinner

Messerschmitt Bf 109T

Strengthened undercarriage legs

Catapult spools both sides

Arrestor hook

imagination, be classed as an 'E'. However, this situation was put right by Matchbox and then Airfix whose model is the best Bf 109E available. The kit enables two versions to be produced, the E-4 (N) Trop and the E-4/B fighter-bomber version.

Made straight from the box the Bf 109 assembles into an accurate replica of the original but there is plenty of scope for the detail fanatic who will want to add internal detail to the cockpit as well as clean up one or two areas, especially around the intakes under the nose. The bucket seat provided is one of the best World War 2-style seats yet produced by Airfix and only requires the back dish to be made slightly more prominent by having the inside ridges smoothed into the general shape. The intakes under the nose should be backed by thin plastic card

and the overall rivet detail slightly reduced but not obliterated altogether. When doing this be careful not to damage the control surfaces as these are particularly well represented.

There are many minor changes which can be made to the basic kit to produce most of the 'E' variants, and reference to such books as William Green's *Augsburg Eagle* and *Messerschmitt Bf 109* in the Classic Aircraft series from Patrick Stephens Ltd make such changes clear. None of the work is as involved as it is, say, for the Spitfire.

One which does require some surgery is the Bf 109T which was designed to be used from aircraft carriers, the 'T' suffix referring to 'Träger' (Carrier). Early in 1939 the German Navy realised the military potential of the aircraft carrier and plans were made to produce two, the

Side view of the Bf 109T showing the solid spinner and hook just forward of the tailwheel.

Messerschmitt Bf 109

Graf Zeppelin and *Peter Strasser,* which they hoped would enable them to make a serious challenge to British sea power. Both carriers were, in fact, laid down, but work was suspended in October 1939, and although it was recommenced in 1942 neither was completed.

At the time the carriers were proposed the Bf 109 was the main Luftwaffe fighter so it was natural that the Messerschmitt design team should turn to this for a suitable aircraft with which to equip the carriers' air groups.

The essential changes were to an E-1 airframe and consisted of adding an arrestor hook aft of the seventh mainframe, catapult spools between the fifth and sixth frames, and an increase in wing area to increase the landing and take-off performance. The wings were arranged to fold just outboard of the armament but this had to be carried out manually and involved detachment of the flaps before it could be done.

The main areas of change to the model are the increase in wingspan, so experience gained with the Bf 109H will be useful, although in this case the method used is entirely different.

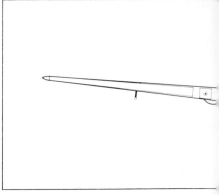

Assemble the fuselage as the kit instructions, not forgetting to blank off the intakes at the nose and add cockpit detail. Build up the arrestor hook fairing on the underside of the fuselage centre-line below the second frame line aft of the hatch marked on the port side. This is done with a small disc of plastic card from which protrudes the arrestor hook made from stretched sprue, the hook terminating just in front of the tail-wheel. The catapult spools are more complicated than those on the Seafire, but again are made from sprue inserted

Plan view of the Bf 109T which shows the increased span.

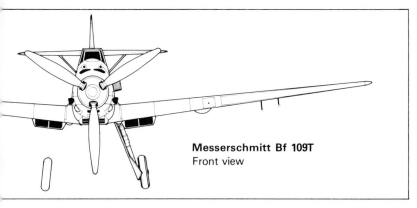

Messerschmitt Bf 109T
Front view

into drilled holes which are angled downwards. The sprue is bent into an 'L' shape with the short leg pointing rearwards. This is done by stretching sprue in the normal way but, whilst it is still warm and pliable, bending it round a suitable former, then plunging it in cold water to set it. Fairings at the base of the spool can be made with the merest touch of filler or a dab of PVA white glue applied with the pointed end of a cocktail stick.

Before assembling the wings, sand off the part numbers from the top sections as these show through the wheel wells, and remove the aileron trim tab from the port wing. Now cement the top and lower sections together and, when they are set, cut off the tips along the line marked outboard of the ailerons. File the cut flat then butt-joint two laminated rectangles of plastic card to the tip areas. These pieces must be at least 3/8-inch long and are best attached with epoxy resin and left to set really hard before any

The Bf 109T and a standard '109E built straight from the Airfix kit, in this case finished as a Tropical version.

Messerschmitt Bf 109

further work is carried out. When the wing extension pieces are set mark the new exteneded tips by continuing the line of the leading and trailing edges, then join these with the new tip line which should be 11/32 inch from the original wings. Cut off the surplus plastic card and sand the new tips to a matching section, using filler where necessary to obtain a neat and continuous extension. The leading edge slots extend to the surface of the added tips as do the ailerons. Addition of the new slots is easily done by cutting them from very thin paper or plastic card and cementing them in place. The ailerons are more difficult as the surface of the ones in the kit should be retained if possible. The best way to do this is to extend the ailerons as shown on the drawings, then take some liquid cement or, or better still, cellulose thinners, and apply this with a brush to the plastic card areas. This must be done with moderation but the result is that the thinners attack the plastic and cause it to 'craze' over and match the kit detail fairly closely. It is best to try this on an odd piece of plastic card first until the technique is mastered. Should you not wish to attempt it, sand all the detail from the kit and simply scribe new ailerons. The wings are now attached to the fuselage, making sure that the di-hederal angle is correct from the wing roots.

Before adding the propeller and spinner, fill the hole in the front of the latter with a small piece of sprue then, with filler, build up a more pointed shape as shown on the drawings. The tailplanes and supporting struts are added as the kit and final small detail, such as aileron mass balances and trim tabs inboard on both ailerons, is added from sprue and plastic card. If you are a real stickler for accuracy you should make slightly greater diameter oleo legs for the main gear as these were strengthened for deck landings. This is a tricky task and is probably best ignored as the difference is slight enough to be of no consequence in this scale.

The canopy in the kit is for an E-4 and is different in framing to that fitted to the E-1 from which the 'T' was derived. To rectify this all that is necessary is to scribe two horizontal lines 1/16 inch from the top on the side panels, and a diagonal line from the front of these on the windscreen to join the moulded frame at the front.

When the carrier programme was shelved the Bf 109T-1 which has been described had all the carrier gear removed, but retained the longer wings, and was fitted with a canopy as provided in the kit. This aircraft, which also had a spinner as supplied in the kit, was used by 1/JG77 (later redesignated 1/JG 5) and operated from Norway where its short field performance proved to be very useful. So if you prefer an operational aircraft, make the T-2 by not adding the catapult spools or arrestor hook, and using the original spinner and canopy.

Colour schemes for the T-1 are, in my experience, non-existent, so the model is best finished in standard Luftwaffe schemes of the period. The T-2, however, can be found with the customary mottle fuselage and splinter wing camouflage and carrying the codes RB + OP. Photographs of one of these aircraft are featured in most of the recommended works on German fighters.

As with the Spitfire, there are many versions of the Messerschmitt which can be made from the vast number of 1:72 scale kits available and these would make into a colourful and interesting collection in their own right.

six

Messerschmitt Me 262B-1a/U1

As the first turbojet-powered aircraft to see operational service, the Me 262 is assured of a place in history and no collection of World War 2 aircraft should be without at least one example. Although designed initially as a fighter, the Me 262 was seen by Hitler as being an ideal aircraft for carrying bombs in retribution for the large-scale bombing raids by the RAF and USAAF. Much against the design team's wishes, they were forced into attempting to adapt the aircraft into a role for which it was completely unsuitable, and by the time it started to reach squadrons in its proper fighter configuration the war was virtually lost.

As well as being produced in many single-seat variants, the Me 262 was also proposed as a two-seat trainer, and from this came a night fighter version which is the subject of this conversion.

The Airfix kit of the Me 262 is again one of their earlier issues but can be improved by adding cockpit detail and refining the surface detail. It is also inexpensive so not a great deal is lost if the conversion is attempted and does not turn out as well as the modeller concerned would have liked.

Start by assembling the fuselage halves, into which is included the nose wheel gear. This means that further work has to be done with this in mind otherwise it is very easy to break the strut off. When the two halves are dry cut the spine off with a fretsaw, starting the cut at the rear of the cockpit and ending it at the base of the fin. If this is done with care both sides should be left with fairly large flat surfaces on their top edges which should also be parallel to each other. When cleaning up the saw cut with a flat file, also file the leading edge of the fin flat as this will have a piece added to it to increase its chord. The tailplane location slots are incorrectly placed and should also be filled with slivers of plastic card and filler at this stage.

A piece of balsa wood the width of the cut area and about 2½ inches long is now firmly bonded to the fuselage, replacing the area that was cut off. This piece of wood must be shaped to fit into the cockpit recess and must also be of sufficient depth for the new fuselage shape. It is better to use a piece which is deeper than needed as it is easier to remove surplus wood than attempt to replace it. It is best to use epoxy glue to bond the balsa to the plastic and advisable to firmly tape or clamp this in

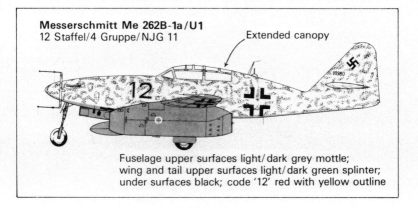

Messerschmitt Me 262B-1a/U1
12 Staffel/4 Gruppe/NJG 11

Extended canopy

Fuselage upper surfaces light/dark grey mottle; wing and tail upper surfaces light/dark green splinter; under surfaces black; code '12' red with yellow outline

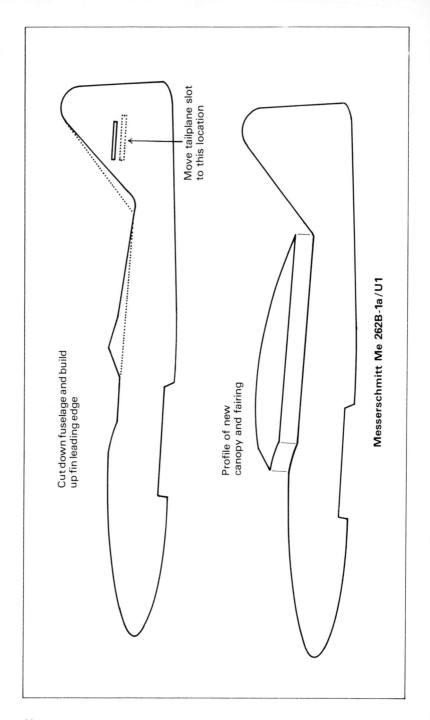

Move tailplane slot to this location

Cut down fuselage and build up fin leading edge

Profile of new canopy and fairing

Messerschmitt Me 262B-1a / U1

These views of the twin-seat Messerschmitt Me 262B-1a/U1 radar-equipped night fighter model clearly show the extensive modifications required to the cockpit area and the 'labour of love' involved in scratch-building the nose aerials unless you are lucky enough to acquire one of the Airmodel conversion kits mentioned in the text.

place whilst it is drying. Leave it for at least 12 hours so that the bond sets really hard and in the meantime assemble the wings and engines as per the kit instructions.

The rear fuselage shape of the two-seat Me 262 is a rather complex one so care is needed in shaping the balsa to the correct section and it is advisable to do it slowly with a sharp knife, making several small cuts instead of a few over-generous ones. The new shape is shown on the plans and when you have nearly achieved this by carving, change to a fairly fine grade of sandpaper for finishing off. Body filler will be needed to merge the balsa into the original plastic and this should also be allowed to set hard before attempts at shaping it are made. When you are satisfied that the shape is correct, mark the outline of the cockpit and remove this by making a vertical cut at the rear with a saw, then along the fuselage line with a sharp knife. The wooden cockpit shape must then be sanded down by the thickness of the acetate which is to be used to mould the canopy. It is then filled with grain filler and polished smooth after which it is attached to a piece of dowelling so that it can be used as a male mould. The shape of the cockpit is then traced on to a strong close-grained piece of balsa and cut out, leaving enough space around the

edges for the male mould to pass through. A piece of acetate sheet is attached to the female former and this is heated under a grill until the acetate is pliable. The male mould is now pushed through and the result should be a clear, accurate canopy. Several attempts might be necessary and be careful not to get the acetate too hot.

Some years ago the German company Airmodel produced a complete moulding for the new canopy and rear spine which can still be obtained from some specialist model shops and save a lot of work if you are lucky enough to find it.

Before adding the canopy, detail the interior by adding instrument panels and seats which will have to be scratch-

Messerschmitt Me 262B-1a/U1

built or obtained from the spares box. A piece of plastic card is added to the leading edge of the fin, increasing its chord at the base and tapering into the pointed top. This is merged into the fin and fuselage with filler and sanded smooth. Grain filler must also be applied to the new balsa sections of the fuselage and it is essential that this is rubbed down between each application and sanded smooth until a glass-like surface is achieved. Before leaving the fuselage, add weight to the nose through the nose wheel door, holding this in place with Plasticine. Suitable weights can be obtained from shops selling fishing equipment or chain stores such as Woolworths who now sell them in handy plastic boxes in a variety of sizes.

Wings, engines and tailplanes are now put in place, the latter being fitted first. These will have to have their locating tongues removed and the root sanded flat then positioned about 1/8 inch below and more forward than the original locating slots, which were filled during the fuselage modifications. This can be tricky as the 'planes must be held accurately in place until they set, so it is as well to look for a fairly quick-drying cement or 5-minute epoxy. Thinner undercarriage doors are made from plastic card and the fork on the nose wheel oleo sanded to a thinner profile.

One of the hardest operations is making and fitting the nose radar array. If you have been lucky enough to obtain the Airmodel conversion kit this is included, but if not, then I am afraid it is a question of stretched sprue, liquid cement and patience. The vertical members should be made from thick flat sprue or cut from 20 thou plastic card sanded to aerofoil section. The horizontal members and their associate vertical aerials are from sprue or toothbrush bristles. The main sections

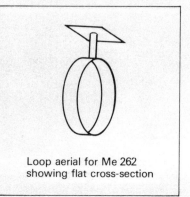

Loop aerial for Me 262 showing flat cross-section

of the array should be fitted into slots cut into the aircraft's nose and the thinner aerials attached after painting, otherwise they will continually be broken off.

The Me 262B-1a was practically always seen with long-range tanks slung on pylons beneath the forward fuselage. The pylons are made from plastic card and the tanks come from a Bf 109 kit. Final detail work is the addition of a D/F loop and radio aerial behind the cockpit. The aerial is made from sprue and the D/F loop is made by cutting a very thin strip from flat plastic card and bending this into a loop around a cocktail stick. This loop was flat in cross section so must not be made from round cross-section stretched sprue.

The model is painted with dark grey and light grey splinter camouflage on the wing and tailplane top surfaces, and light grey with medium grey mottle on the fuselage. All undersurfaces are matt black, extending back along the leading edges of the top wing surfaces. All insignia are of the simplified type except the swastika which is solid black; the code number '10' on the nose is red outlined white.

seven

Messerschmitt Me 163 Komet

Among the many revolutionary designs proposed, and in some cases built, for the Luftwaffe, the rocket-powered Me 163 fighter is the best-known and most successful. Designed by Professor Alexander Lippisch, who is famous for his many unconventional tailless gliders, the Me 163 is still the only purely rocket-powered aircraft to have served with any air force. Pushed into service long before many of its design snags could be ironed out, the Me 163 was not an outstanding success and claimed the lives of many Luftwaffe pilots. In very simple terms, the aircraft was very much a lightweight fighter which could climb at a phenomenal rate on a very short engine run, during which it was uncatchable by contemporary Allied fighters. When the motor cut, it could maintain a fair speed and degree of manoeuvrability, but

Two views of the diminutive Me 163B built straight from the Airfix kit with no modification.

during the descent it was tricky to fly and extremely vulnerable, especially in the landing approach when the lack of any form of motive power prevented it from overshooting or taking any real form of evasive action. The fuel used by its rocket motor was extremely volatile and unstable, resulting in the loss of a number of pilots when it exploded for no apparent reason. Armed with two wing root-mounted 20 mm (later 30 mm) cannons, it packed a lethal punch which could be used to advantage during its period of high speed interception, but post-war records show that it did not, in fact, achieve the 'kill' rate often claimed for it.

Nevertheless, the Me 163 was potentially a menacing weapon and although it is arguable whether or not the concept of a rocket-powered fighter—even with modern-day technology—is a worthwhile project (the

lack of any serious development seemingly proving that it is not) the diminutive German fighter is a 'must' for inclusion in any serious study of World War 2 model aircraft.

The release in 1977 of a 1:72 scale kit by Airfix is bound to see an upsurge in interest in this aircraft, as prior to this no accurate 1:72 scale models were available.

Measurements of the Airfix kit scale out exactly right and assembled as it comes the builder will be rewarded with a fine model, so there are only one or two pointers to be looked for in detailing which will generally improve the model.

Cockpit areas are nearly always places where improvement can be carried out and the Me 163 is no exception. Airfix provide a floor to which is attached a seat, headrest, control column and instrument panel. The latter should have the instruments moulded to it removed as these are fictional in quantity and position, being more akin to the Me 163A (Anton) than the B version depicted by the kit. Instrumentation was very simple and

consisted of six basic instruments on a centre panel, this being shown in the model as carrying two instruments only. There were three instruments to the right in a vertical spread and a sub-panel above the centre one and below the gun sight. Small pieces of plastic card are used to build up the sub-panels and side consoles, and the instruments, switches lights, etc, painted on these. The very small size means that a touch of paint will be sufficient to represent the panels, but it is worth doing this as the canopy is so clear that their absence is very noticeable. Safety straps from paper are added to the seat which can also be improved by having sides added to it from five thou plastic card.

An armoured glass screen and gun sight must be added to the forward cockpit coaming, and if the model is to be made with its canopy open, remember that this hinged sideways on the starboard side and the whole bubble lifted.

One of the aircraft for which decals are provided, number 10 of 2/JG 400, was fitted with a D/F loop aft of the

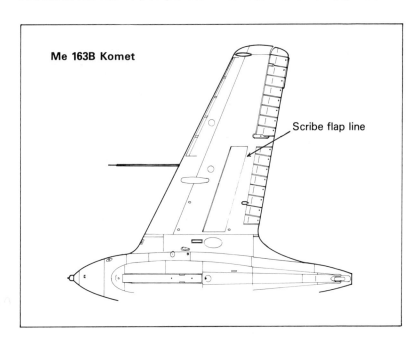

Me 163B Komet

Scribe flap line

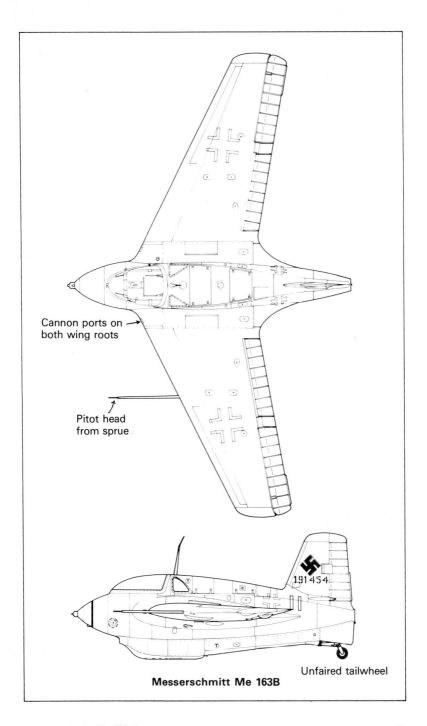

Cannon ports on
both wing roots

Pitot head
from sprue

191454

Messerschmitt Me 163B

Unfaired tailwheel

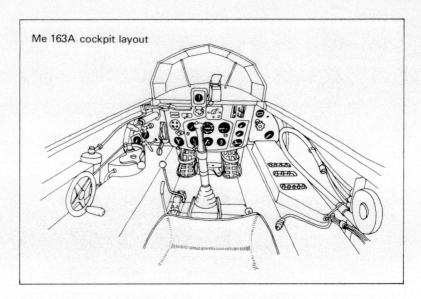

Me 163A cockpit layout

main aerial, the position of this being ½ inch to the rear of the aerial on the centre-line. The loop is made from sprue as previously described and fitted to a small fairing made from card or filler.

If the model is made with its skid lowered, the tailwheel should also be shown in the lowered position, this being achieved by cutting the front location point at an angle and inserting a supporting strut between the lowered leg and the fuselage. The kit provides both a faired and unfaired tailwheel, the latter being more commonly seen on operational aircraft.

When the model has been assembled, drill two holes in the wing roots to represent the 20 mm cannons, these being at the halfway point on the root fairing moulded to the fuselage. A different colour scheme than that suggested in the kit is the all-red Me 163B-OV 41 of Major Späte, this being illustrated in Profile No 225.

This aircraft has protruding barrels for its cannons and these are represented by stretched sprue.

The spent ammunition chutes on the underside of the wing roots, just forward of the domed inspection panels are slightly too wide, so for greater accuracy it is best to fill them and scribe new ones; similarly the scriber can be used to outline the large flaps which were located on the undersides of the Me 163 wings and are not shown on the Airfix model.

Cockpit interior is light grey (RLM Grau 02) and most instruments were black-faced. The most commonly seen camouflage pattern consisted of light blue (Hellblau 65) on undersides of wings, fuselage and tail surfaces; fuselage sides and fin/rudder oversprayed in light grey mottle (RLM Grau 02); top wing surfaces in splinter camouflage of dark green (Dunkelgrün 71) and black green (Schwarzgrün 70). There were, of course, other variations which the individual who wants something different will be quite capable of finding for himself.

eight

Mitsubishi A6M Zero-Sen

The Zero-Sen is as well known among World War 2 fighters as the Spitfire and Bf 109, and the passage of time has done little to tarnish the reputation it established for itself during the early days of the war. The myth surrounding the Zero started in the early days of the Pacific war when it achieved complete superiority over its adversaries, and its appearance over Pearl Harbour caused the Americans much heart-searching. In its day it was the first carrier-borne fighter to surpass the performance of shored-based fighters, and its high performance, coupled with superb manoeuvrability, quickly enabled it to establish its supremacy in every major air battle in which it took part. It was not until an almost intact Zero was captured by the Americans that its legend of invincibility became dented, as several shortcomings in its design were discovered.

Like its two contemporaries mentioned earlier, the Zero underwent many major and minor design changes and was produced in a bewildering number of versions, which are too numerous to become involved with in this book. More Zeros were produced than any other Japanese warplane and, although its fortunes declined as better Allied fighters were introduced, it stayed in service until the end of the war and is still the most famous of all Japanese-produced fighter aircraft.

The Airfix kit of the Zero represents an A6M2, which was the first version to be produced in quantity and the basic type used at Pearl Harbour and during the early Pacific campaign. To be absolutely precise the full designation of this aircraft was A6M2 Type 21; its predecessor being the A6M2 Type 11,

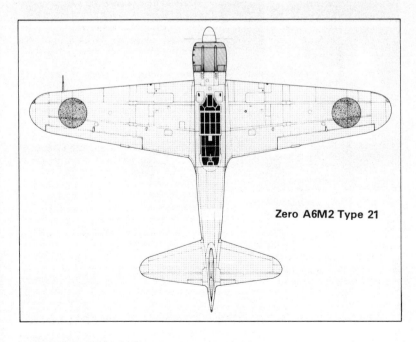

Zero A6M2 Type 21

A6M2 Zero made from the Hasegawa kit, modified to show the canopy open. This is a much later release than the Airfix kit of the same aircraft and makes an interesting comparison with the older offering.

Another view of the A6M2, this time with canopy closed.

the difference being that the type 21 had folding wing tips and carrier equipment. The name Zero, by the way, was used because production models of the Navy aircraft were assigned type numbers based on the last number of the Japanese year in which they were evolved; 1940 was the year 2600 in the Japanese calendar therefore the A6M

series was known as the Zero, or Type 0 Carrier Fighter.

The modeller who wishes to use Airfix kits exclusively for his collection of World War 2 fighters is faced with many problems when it comes to the Zero. The kit is one of the oldest produced by the company and has many shortcomings, some of which it is impossible to correct without major surgery.

In view of the fact that there are now much newer and more accurate kits available, the reader could well be excused for asking the question 'Why bother with the Airfix offering?'. There is no answer that will satisfy everyone, but one valid reason is quite logical, even if the modeller who wishes to use no other manufacturers' kits is discounted. Airfix kits are readily available to all modellers and it is therefore not necessary to have to wait for supplies of others from a variety of sources, but more important is the fact that every serious modeller will at some time be faced with the task of carrying out major conversions. The feel of working in plastic can therefore be obtained quite easily and inexpensively by practising on such kits as the Zero, where not a great deal is lost if things go wrong. The notes on the Zero are therefore aimed at such modellers, whilst others who do not wish to become involved in such matters can happily produce their Japanese fighters by building other kits, such as the Hasegawa range, straight from the box.

Basically the Airfix kit is incorrect in the fuselage since the cockpit is too far forward, the fuselage is too wide in cross section, too deep in front of the fin and the wrong shape at the rear end. The cowling is clumsy and the tailplanes far too short in span. Having said all that it becomes obvious that a completely new fuselage is required, but this is perhaps going to too great an extreme, so we must look at ways of improving what we have.

The first step is to provide a sound basis on which cockpit interior detail can be added, and this is done by inserting a floor made from a piece of

Modelling World War 2 Fighters

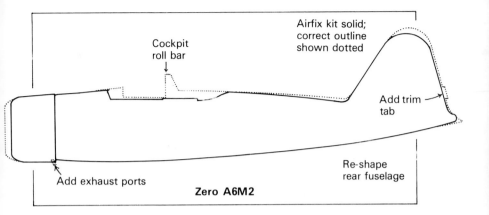

Cockpit
roll bar

Airfix kit solid;
correct outline
shown dotted

Add trim
tab

Add exhaust ports

Re-shape
rear fuselage

Zero A6M2

plastic card 1 7/16 inches long and 9/16 inch wide, tapering at the rear end to meet the fuselage contours. Side consoles and an instrument panel are added, together with a scratch-built bucket seat, control column and rudder pedals. A roll bar must also be made from sprue and this will be fitted behind the pilot's head, but it is advisable to leave it off at this stage. Before inserting the cockpit detail, the fuselage can be sanded so as to reduce its width on a flat piece of wet and dry fixed to a board. Both sides should be reduced by the same amount but don't overdo this otherwise problems in fitting will occur. However, even a small amount removed from both halves will improve the overall appearance.

When the two halves are fitted together and thoroughly dry, the width just forward of the fin/rudder is reduced by sanding with wet and dry. Make sure that material is removed from the top and bottom and take special care to ensure that the sanding does not result in flat areas. The rear end aft of the rudder must be reshaped as shown on the drawing and the top rear section of the rudder reduced in height as well as being made more rounded. Apart from a major rebuild there is little which can be done about the position of the cockpit, but this can be improved and given a more accurate appearance by increasing the length of the cowling — which is too short

anyway. This is done by cutting two circular discs from 20 thou plastic card to the same diameter as the rear section of the cowling and cementing these in place on it. If you feel so inclined, the moulded engine can also be removed at this stage and replaced with a better one from the spares box, taking care to cement this firmly in place before the plastic card discs are added.

The cowling with the discs in place is then cemented to the fuselage and the additions sanded to meet the fuselage contours. The gap left between the fuselage and cowling where the original location area for the former is moulded, is covered by cooling gills made from 5 thou plastic card, either individually or in the form of a scribed strip. Don't forget to extend the machine-gun troughs through the plastic card additions and whilst doing this clean up the flat area in which the guns are located on the fuselage. This is too wide on the kit and not very well defined, but the original reduction in width will have improved this and the sides can be made more angular and prominent with a small flat file. These additions to the cowling will mean that the fuselage is now slightly too long in scale, but will result in a better scale appearance as far as cockpit positioning is concerned.

The intake under the nose must now be improved in shape by being sanded to more rounded contours and having its lips reshaped with a sharp knife to

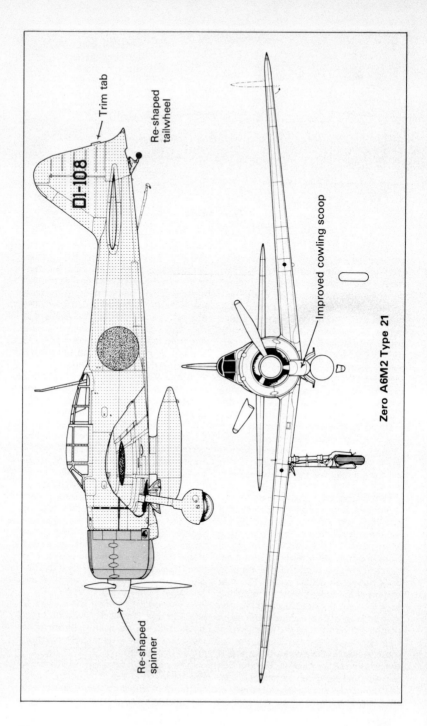

Trim tab

Re-shaped
tailwheel

DI-108

Re-shaped
spinner

Improved cowling scoop

Zero A6M2 Type 21

Modelling World War 2 Fighters

give a sharper line to its interior edges. In the Airfix kit the tailwheel assembly is a bit of a disaster, matched only by the arrestor hook, and ideally both should be replaced. If you have not yet accumulated enough spare parts, they can still be greatly improved by reducing the boat-shaped blister to which the wheel is attached, and thinning down the hook.

Unfortunately the propeller and spinner are also rather poor, the blades being the wrong shape and the spinner too blunt. Replacement presents a major problem, the easiest method being to cut the blades from the spinner then reshape this with filler before adding new broader-chord blades from plastic card. The faint at heart can compromise by simply making the spinner longer by adding filler, and putting up with the original blades.

Turning to the wings, it will be found that these are accurate in chord and span but rather heavily detailed. Attention from wet and dry will soon put this right but before fixing the two halves together, enlarge the wheel wells, giving the actual area into which the wheels retract a more rounded shape. The wells should also be given walls made from thin strips of plastic card, this work being carried out before final assembly. The wheels themselves are very marginally oversize in diameter but it is not really worth loosing any sleep in putting these right. Thinner wheel doors from plastic card and a reduction in thickness of the oleo fork,

during which the outer sides are sanded flat, improves the under-carriage of the Zero which should not be fitted until the final detail work on the completed airframe has been completed.

The last major task is the replace-ment of the kit tailplanes, which are too short in span, with new ones made from plastic card of suitable thickness. When all this work has been com-pleted, add the roll bar as well as two exhaust ports from stretched sprue. The latter are located either side of the scoop under the cowling and protrude at an outward-pointing angle from the cowling gills. A radio aerial is made from a strip of flat plastic card and fitted through the canopy which, by the way, is about 1/5 inch too long. This fault can only be put right by moulding a new canopy and this will in turn lead to problems in location on the fuselage, so it is perhaps best to accept it as it is. Zeros were invariably seen with the under fuselage fuel tank *in situ* so this must be cemented in place. Unfortun-ately it is too short so should be extended by the addition of a plastic card insert behind the moulded pylon, or replaced completely by another from the spares box if the right shape can be found.

The result of all this effort will be a model which is better looking than one made straight from the box, but it will still not be 100 per cent accurate. However, it will have been a test of modelling skills and help the inex-

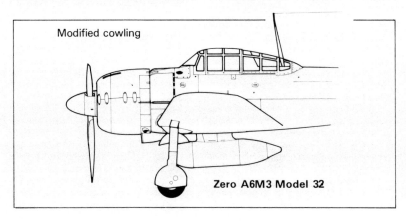

Modified cowling

Zero A6M3 Model 32

Two views of the A6M3 Type 32, basically a clipped-wing Zero. The modified cowling and spinner are just two of the many necessary modifications required to produce an acceptable Zero from the now rather aged Airfix kit.

perienced to acquire some of these at a modest cost. If the work is done carefully there will also be the added bonus of a model which, when compared with the original boxed kit, will show just what can be done in modelling terms with comparatively poor basic material.

There were many different versions of the Zero and most of the later ones would be quite impossible to construct from the Airfix kit, but there are two which can be, and will add a little variety.

The easiest is the A6M3 Model 32, which was basically a clipped-wing version of the A6M2 Type 21 just

described. To construct this version carry out all the improvements already described for the basic kit, modifying them where necessary as follows.

The A6M3 had a different engine, the most noticeable change being the deletion of the air scoop under the cowling (Part 9). Omission of this part means that the cowling must be built up at the front with body filler and the flat area underneath, where it locates, rounded off by sanding. A new intake was located inside the cowling at the top and this is represented by a strip of plastic card cemented inside the cowling at the top, parallel to the horizontal centre-line. This will look much more convincing if the moulded engine is removed and the forward cowling lip thinned down and made more rounded in side profile.

The wing tips are cut off just outside the engraved panel line, making sure that the outer line of the ailerons is not disturbed. Wet and dry is then used to round off the new square tips to correct section.

One of the most challenging versions of the Zero is the A6M2-N floatplane, or 'Rufe', as it was known. Some years ago the Japanese company LS marketed a kit of this aircraft in 1:72 scale, but it does in fact measure out to 1:75 scale which is enough to make it look entirely out of place alongside a 1:72 scale Zero. However, this kit is still

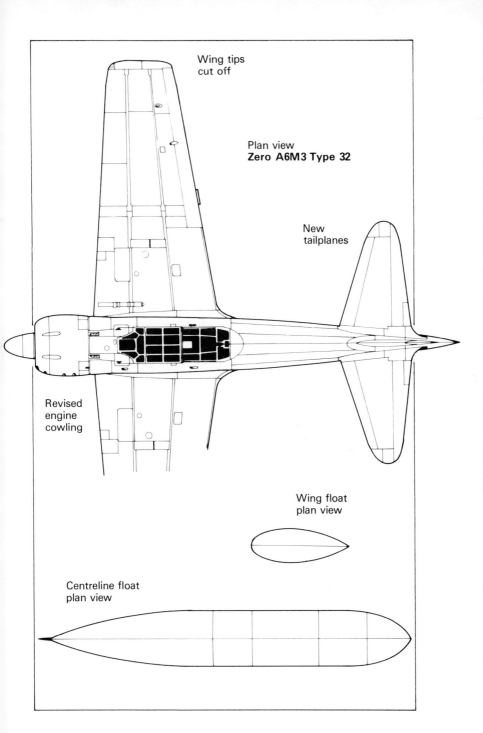

Wing tips
cut off

Plan view
Zero A6M3 Type 32

New
tailplanes

Revised
engine
cowling

Wing float
plan view

Centreline float
plan view

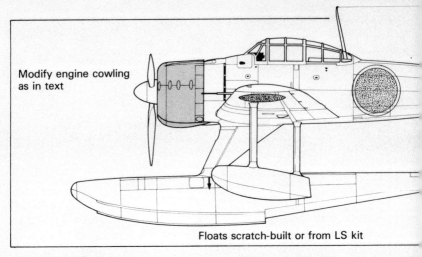

Modify engine cowling as in text

Floats scratch-built or from LS kit

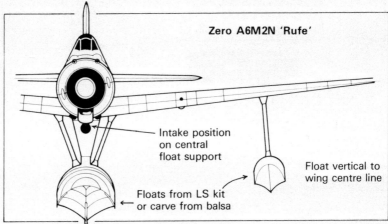

Zero A6M2N 'Rufe'

Intake position
on central
float support

Float vertical to
wing centre line

Floats from LS kit
or carve from balsa

readily available and the floats are near enough in scale to be used, thus saving a lot of hard toil in carving new ones.

Once again the work outlined for the original A6M2 must be carried out, but this time be sure to use Part 9 while omitting Part 13. Before assembling the wings, add a plastic card filler across the wheel wells then fill these with putty which is sanded until it blends with the underside shape of the wing sections. The Rufe had a rudder of greater area than the Zero so also remove this from the kit and make a new one from plastic card, the same material also being used to make the sub-fin under the fuselage beneath the

fin/rudder. This is made in two sections, one being fixed to the rudder and the other to the fuselage, and is located over the hole where the hook and tailwheel fit. This hole is filled with odd pieces of sprue held in place with filler then carved and sanded to shape.

The intake represented by Part 13 was located in the top of the central float support and is shown on the LS components. It can be improved by drilling out and having a small piece of hollow tubing inserted into it; this must be flush with the leading edge of the float support. The large central float is aligned on the aircraft's centre-line and care must be taken to ensure that it is

Y2-102

↑
Add sub-fin

Zero A6M2-N 'Rufe'

Two views of the A6M2-N 'Rufe' modified from the Airfix Zero, clearly showing how the enormous central float extended well beyond the aircraft's nose.

perfectly vertical when viewed from the front. This component from the LS kit fits the Airfix Zero almost perfectly but it will be found necessary to add filler to its rear end otherwise an unsightly gap wil remain. The wing floats are from the same source and fit on the main spar 1 9/32 inches from the tip and ¼ inch from the leading edge. When viewed from the front the wing floats point outwards, the correct angle being obtained by making their horizontal axis parallel to the dihedral of the wing; in side view the support struts are vertical.

If difficulty is experienced in obtaining a LS Rufe kit, the only alternative — at the time of writing — is to scratch-build all the floats from balsa and their supports from plastic card. The completed model will stand quite well on its centre float although it does lean on the step, but a beaching trolley comprising a cradle on two wheels can easily be constructed from scrap, or the model displayed on a Polyfilla sea.

As with all the models featured there are many colour schemes available to the modeller who is prepared to look for

Mitsubishi A6M Zero-Sen

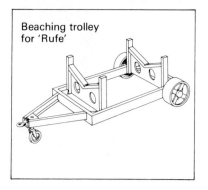

Beaching trolley
for 'Rufe'

grey or natural metal overall (this being fairly rare) with black cowlings. Later the grey was frequently covered in dark green splodges which gave way to dark green on all top surfaces with light grey retained underneath, the cowlings usually being left black. Similar schemes were also used on the Rufe although some publications show this to have been pained in a peculiar mauve finish for which there is little supporting evidence. Propeller blades were usually silver on their front surfaces and black or dark brown on their rear, they also frequently had two red lines at their tips. Interior colour was a pale sickly green with matt black panels and consoles, but towards the end of the war natural metal interiors were very much in evidence.

them, so one appropriate to the general period being modelled must be selected by the individual to suit his own needs. In general terms Japanese Navy aircraft were not usually as colourful as their Army Air Force counterparts, the most usual finishes being grey/green, overall grey or training school orange.

During the early stages of the Pacific war the Zero was often finished light

The serious modeller of Japanese aircraft will find that Letraset sheets numbers 44 to 47 contain a wealth of interesting unit and national markings which will go a long way to improving any model of the Zero or Rufe.

Vought F4U-1D Corsair

nine

little over two years since its first action with VMF-124 at Guadalcanal in February 1943.

Throughout its service life the Corsair underwent many changes, ranging from the replacement of the first 'birdcage' cockpit canopy—which restricted its use from carriers in the F4U-1 version—to a blown bubble hood, detail alterations to the airframe, armament, propeller and cowling. Despite such attention it always retained the original, somewhat sinister-looking, shape which is perhaps the key to its popularity among modellers.

The aircraft represented by the Airfix kit is a F4U-1D and provides a good accurate basis from which many

One of the most distinctive features of the Chance-Vought F4U series of Corsair fighters was the peculiar cranked wing which had marked anhedral from the fuselage to the main undercarriage legs, then dihedral to the tips. This powerful and very successful fighter, which was used by the US Navy and Marines, the Fleet Air Arm and other forces, has always been a popular modelling subject and one which lends itself to many interesting and simple conversions.

The Corsair first flew in May 1940 and was destined to give service not only in World War 2 but also the Korean war, where legend has it that sons of World War 2 Corsair pilots flew the same aircraft that their fathers had in the earlier conflict!

By the time the Japanese surrendered, the Corsair had accounted for over 2,100 Japanese aircraft in the Pacific Theatre against a loss of only 189, this success being achieved in a

A Corsair F4U-1 made from the Airfix and Frog kits. This is an aircraft of VF17 flown by Lieutenant Freeman. The cooling gills missing from the Airfix kit can be seen to the rear of the cowling.

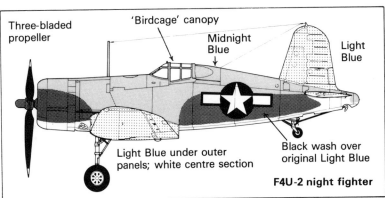

Three-bladed propeller

'Birdcage' canopy

Midnight Blue

Light Blue

Light Blue under outer panels; white centre section

Black wash over original Light Blue

F4U-2 night fighter

Two views of the F4U-2 night fighter model with 'birdcage' canopy and radar nacelle on the starboard wing.

different versions can be constructed. The kit is what one can term a 'second generation' Airfix model, being one (big) step beyond the simple parts of the company's very first productions but not quite as refind as present-day offerings. The addition of cockpit detail, replacing the seat and pilot provided with a proper floor, instrument panel, side consoles and control column, is an obvious starting point. The rather heavy surface detail, which is dominated by a surfeit of rivets, should also be refined, and the cowling can be greatly improved by having its front edges slightly thinned and rounded, as well as the scribing of cooling gills which have been completely omitted.

Before constructing the model it is best to remove all the rivet detail by sanding but before doing this make a note of the position of panels engraved on the wings and fuselage as these will need to be re-scribed. The sanding operation should be carried out carefully so that damage does not occur to the control surfaces, as these are well represented on the mouldings. Scribing the cooling gills is tricky and is best done by covering the front section of the cowling with a strip of masking tape which should extend back to a line of 1/8 inch from the rear. The exposed area, which will be 1/8 inch strip round the total diameter, is the space occupied by the gills. A sharp scriber is gently run around the edge of the masking tape and when this is removed a perfect demarcation line should result. Individual gills are then marked around the cowling as shown on the drawings. Since these gills were designed to open, it is possible to cut them from thin plastic card or writing paper and cement them in the open position, which will certainly improve the model but will become very much a labour of love as every gill must be identical if the model is to look right.

Before assembling the wing halves,

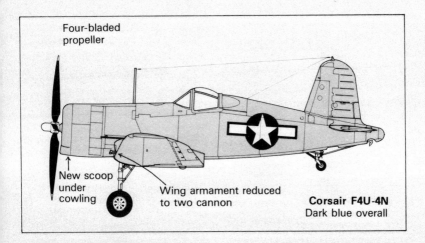

Four-bladed propeller

New scoop under cowling

Wing armament reduced to two cannon

Corsair F4U-4N
Dark blue overall

remove the locating points around the two outer edges of the wheel wells; these being included to locate the doors in the closed position; then build-up an internal well with strips of plastic card.

The machine-gun ports in the wing should have a small drill passed through them to give a better definition, and barrels from stretched sprue will not look out of place recessed into them. The propeller boss has a web of plastic joining the blades at their roots and this must be removed with a sharp knife, but make sure that the individual blade's pitch mechanism, a round base, is not interfered with. Thinning down of the undercarriage doors, sprue aerials and arrestor hook and attention to many of the finer points which, by now, should be second nature, will result in a very acceptable model from an inexpensive kit.

One of the most popular versions frequently chosen by British modellers is the Corsair II used by the Fleet Air Arm, but many fall into the trap of simply painting the model in Royal Navy colours. This version, whilst basically remaining an F4U-1, had some subtle changes, the most noticeable of which was the removal of 16 inches from each wing tip to permit below-deck stowage on British carriers, so if you chose this version don't forget to carry out this most essential modification.

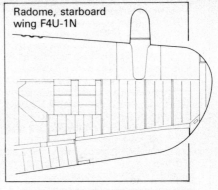

Radome, starboard wing F4U-1N

One distinction which went to the Corsair was that of being the first radar-carrying single-seat night fighter to see operational service, this version being the F4U-2. This modification is fairly simple although it does involve fitting the earlier 'birdcage' canopy. To do this, before assembling the fuselage halves, cut off the pointed moulded protrusion at the top rear of the cockpit opening, then, when the halves are joined, insert a balsa block into the opening. This block is now carved to the shape of the original flat-topped canopy, carefully cut off, and used to mould a new one. When this has been made it is fitted in place and frame lines painted or applied with thin strips of correctly coloured tape.

The airborne radar was housed in a bullet-shaped fairing on the starboard

Vought F4U-1D Corsair

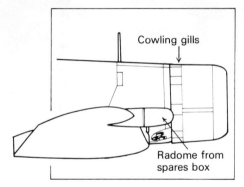

Cowling gills

Radome from
spares box

wing and this component is made from a suitable drop tank or a similar component from another kit. The scanner fairing from an Airfix Firefly (Parts 62, 63 and 64) can be modified fairly easily to fit the Corsair wing and is, in fact, easier to use if you feel that the expense in obtaining another kit is justified. Once again the absence of suitable parts in the spares box need not be a deterrent as the radar pod can be carved from balsa or built up with filler over a plastic card former.

On this version of the Corsair the standard wing armament was retained but aerial locations tended to vary as did their styles. Reference to photographs, which should be an essential part of research before any model is constructed, will provide the answers. The other work mentioned in refining the original kit must also be carried out but in addition to this, remove the bomb pylons which are moulded to the inboard sections of the wings.

Although the F4U-4N night fighter was too late to see service in World War

2 it is a natural progression and worthy of attention.

This aircraft had the wing armament reduced to two guns in each wing, but these were cannons rather than machine-guns so the firepower was increased. The major change for this model is the addition of a scoop under the cowling, this being built up from plastic card and filler as was done for the Hurricane tropical filters described earlier. The three-bladed propeller must also be replaced with a four-bladed one and a radar scanner pod added to the starboard wing. Aerials appeared in a variety of places but when studying photographs to locate these make sure you are, in fact, looking at an F4U-4N and not a -5N. The two look similar but the -5 was very much a post-war version and had many other changes including two intakes either side of the cowling instead of one underneath, these not always being noticeable from certain angles. It also had a wider fuselage forward of the cockpit and a different exhaust arrangement. This would also be a challenging conversion but beyond the scope and space currently available in this book.

Colour schemes for Navy and Marine Corsairs are plentiful, ranging from the two-tone blue and white commonly seen on a lot of models, to the light grey overall finish now familiar on present day US Navy and Marine aircraft. In between there are overall midnight blue aircraft, many of which sported a variety of coloured fuselage and cowling bands. Profiles number 47 and 150, as well as Aircam number 23, should provide sufficient inspiration even to the most demanding Corsair connoisseur.